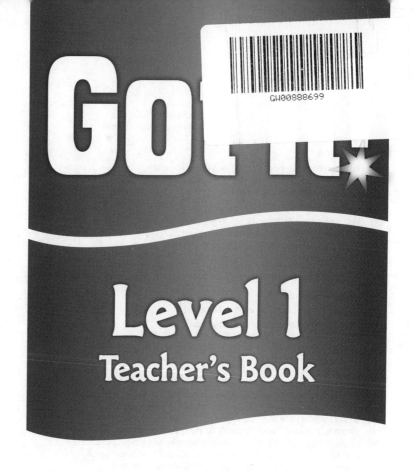

Got It!

Level 1
Teacher's Book

Claire Thacker

OXFORD
UNIVERSITY PRESS

OXFORD
UNIVERSITY PRESS

Great Clarendon Street, Oxford OX2 6DP

Oxford University Press is a department of the University of Oxford.
It furthers the University's objective of excellence in research, scholarship,
and education by publishing worldwide in

Oxford New York

Auckland Cape Town Dar es Salaam Hong Kong Karachi
Kuala Lumpur Madrid Melbourne Mexico City Nairobi
New Delhi Shanghai Taipei Toronto

With offices in

Argentina Austria Brazil Chile Czech Republic France Greece
Guatemala Hungary Italy Japan Poland Portugal Singapore
South Korea Switzerland Thailand Turkey Ukraine Vietnam

OXFORD and OXFORD ENGLISH are registered trade marks of
Oxford University Press in the UK and in certain other countries

Contents

Introduction

Teaching notes

Workbook answer key

Introduction

Introducing *Got it!*

Methodology

Got it! is a new four-level American English course written specifically for secondary school students, with particular emphasis on meaningful communication and skills development.

Key features of the methodology are:

Hands-on language presentation. Students immediately interact with the dialogue or text that opens each unit, checking their understanding of meaning and context, and giving them the chance to try out new structures;

Guided discovery. Students explore the meaning and usage of new language before they move on to more formal presentation and practice;

Communicative practice. Dialogue work and personalization are emphasized at each level, and pairwork activities and games are included throughout;

Cultural awareness. A focus on the U.S. and other English-speaking countries is placed within the context of the wider world;

Skills development. In every unit students apply and extend what they have learned, through targeted skills lessons designed to build their competence in each individual skill;

Self-assessment. Students regularly review and measure their progress against the Common European Framework of Reference;

Learning across the curriculum. Inter-disciplinary reading and project pages link the topics and language content of the main units to other areas of the school curriculum;

Values. The topics in *Got it!* have been carefully chosen to stimulate reflection on a broad range of issues related to citizenship and the development of socially responsible values. These are highlighted in the teaching notes for each unit.

Flexibility

A comprehensive and innovative package of components gives the teacher maximum support and flexibility. Whatever your teaching style, *Got it!* has everything you could possibly need to match your students' learning environment.

Combined Student Book and Workbook, available in full and split editions;

Student CD-ROM, with many hours of interactive material for home practice, including extra listening activities;

iTools, featuring a fully interactive Student Book and Workbook, for use in class with an interactive whiteboard, computer or data projector;

Video, with four cultural documentaries and worksheets per level, available on DVD (with additional on-screen comprehension questions), or to launch from projectable worksheets on the iTools disc;

Flexible assessment options. Printable, editable tests are included on the iTools disc, while the Print Test Generator allows you to create and edit randomized tests of your own;

KET and PET practice tests for levels 2 and 3 of *Got it!* Each iTools contains a printable practice test; the Student CD-ROM gives students access to a fully supported interactive online practice test. Further practice tests can be purchased from oxfordenglishtesting.com;

Printable worksheets. 50 extra worksheets are included on each iTools, including pairwork activities and games, and review and extension worksheets for extra grammar and vocabulary practice;

Interactive content. Extra video and audio material for use with a Learning Management System.

Overview of components

Student Book and Workbook

The Student Book contains:

- eight teaching units;
- a Welcome unit, reviewing key language from the previous level. In the Starter level, the Welcome unit briefly reviews basic language typically covered at primary level;
- a Remember unit for mid-year language review and consolidation. In the split edition of *Got it!*, the Remember unit opens the second volume at each level;
- vocabulary and grammar review after every two units;
- a Culture club lesson in each Review unit, providing an insight into life in the U.S. and other English-speaking countries;
- regular My progress self-assessment pages correlated to the Common European Framework of Reference;
- four Curriculum extra reading and project lessons.

The Workbook contains:

- additional practice for each teaching unit, covering grammar, vocabulary, communication, reading, and writing;
- detailed grammar notes and wordlists, included at the start of each Workbook unit for ease of reference.

Student CD-ROM

The Student CD-ROM contains:

- extra interactive practice for each vocabulary, grammar, and communication lesson from the Student Book;
- extra listening practice;
- interactive games;
- free access to an interactive online KET or PET practice test (*Got it!* levels 2 and 3 only).

iTools

iTools is designed to be used in the classroom with an interactive whiteboard. It can also be used with a computer linked to a monitor or data projector. Features include:

- fully interactive Student Book content including full class audio;
- answer keys and audio scripts which can be turned on or off;
- extra audio to accompany reading texts in Skills lessons;
- complete Workbook contents with answer keys;
- the ability to alternate between corresponding Student Book and Workbook pages at the touch of a button;
- four video lessons containing complete video clips; students can view the video clips with or without scripts;
- 50 printable worksheets, which can also be projected in class, including pairwork, games, and language review and extension;
- editable tests for every unit;
- a printable KET practice test for *Got it!* level 2, and a printable PET practice test for level 3;

DVD

Video material for *Got it!* is also available on two DVDs. The DVDs contain:

- four cultural documentaries per level, linked to the topical and linguistic content of the Student Book;
- on-screen interactive comprehension questions;
- printable worksheets for each documentary;
- teaching notes with full scripts and answer keys.

Test Builder

The Test Builder contains a large database of questions in a variety of activity formats, allowing you to:

- select questions by length, format, and language point;
- create as many different tests as you like, with just a few clicks of the mouse;
- edit your tests, add your own material, print the tests, and save on your computer for future use.

Interactive content

Interactive content, for use with a Learning Management System. The content for each level includes:

- extra interactive listening practice;
- extra interactive video content.

Teacher's Book

The Teacher's Book contains:

- teaching notes and answer keys for all the Student Book material;
- ideas for warm-ups and extra activities;
- suggestions for using authentic songs with specific topics or areas of language;
- background notes and cultural information on people and topics mentioned in the Student Book;
- audio scripts for listening material;
- a Workbook answer key.

Class Audio CDs

Each set of Class Audio CDs contains:

- all the listening material for the Student Book;
- listening test audio.

Using the Student Book

Welcome unit

The Welcome unit offers six pages of vocabulary and grammar practice, covering language students have seen in the previous level. In the Starter level, students are given a brief overview of basic language they may have seen at primary level, before beginning the main syllabus in unit 1.

Main units

Presentation

The presentation text on the left hand page exposes students to the theme, grammar, vocabulary, and functions of the unit. The exercises on the right hand page allow students to interact with the dialogue or text in more detail, encouraging them to explore, use, and personalize new language before it is formally presented and practiced on the Vocabulary and Grammar pages.

In the Starter level and level 1, the text is a dialogue presented in a photostory format. The photostories reflect the aspirations of students, using familiar contexts to motivate and engage them. Each unit focuses on a different episode in the lives of the central characters.

In the Starter level, the story takes place in a performing arts school and follows the fortunes of a new student, Holly. Holly is happy to be at her new school and quickly makes friends, but she also finds that she has a rival who wants to prevent her from achieving her dreams. The story culminates in the production of a school musical, where Holly finally wins the lead role.

In level 1, we follow the story of Sam. Sam loves basketball, but he is having problems with poor grades in his other school subjects. As he faces a moral dilemma, he is helped by a friend to make the right choice, and in the end everything works out for the best.

In levels 2 and 3, the emphasis is on texts dealing with individual topics of a more grown-up nature, in recognition of the fact that students, along with their interests and tastes, mature very quickly during the teenage years. A variety of formats and genres is used, including dialogues, magazine articles, and web pages.

Following on from the presentation text, students complete a series of questions to check basic comprehension. The **Check it out!** feature (in Starter level and Level 1 only) draws students' attention to useful colloquial expressions in the dialogue.

Language focus

The exercises in the Language focus section familiarize students with the language of the unit, without requiring them to manipulate it. In Starter and level 1, students focus on the target language in relation to specific scenes and sections of dialogue from the photostory; in levels 2 and 3, students find phrases and structures in the presentation text and use them to complete sentences or captions about the text.

Finally, **Focus on you** and **Pairwork** activities give students the chance to try out the new language in a personalized context, following carefully controlled models.

Vocabulary

This page presents and practices a set of vocabulary items associated with the unit topic and previewed in the presentation lesson. **Look!** boxes contain useful tips and draw attention to potential pitfalls, including spelling rules, exceptions or irregular forms, collocations, and notes about English usage.

Students once again have the opportunity for guided speaking practice with a **Pairwork** activity at the end of the lesson.

At the foot of the Vocabulary page, students are directed to the Student CD-ROM and the Workbook, where there is further practice of the unit vocabulary.

Grammar

Underlying the methodology of *Got it!* is the conviction that students understand and remember rules better if they work them out for themselves. As a result, a guided discovery approach to teaching grammar is adopted throughout the series.

Each unit has two Grammar lessons. A grammar chart models the form of the key structures. Having already experimented with the new structures earlier in the unit, students are encouraged to reflect on correct usage in more detail as they complete the **Think!** activity.

A cross-reference to **Rules** then directs the students to a grammar reference page in the corresponding Workbook unit, where detailed explanations and examples are given.

The activities on the page provide thorough and detailed practice of both form and usage, moving from carefully controlled exercises to more demanding production.

Each Grammar page has an optional **Finished?** activity. These are designed as a fun way of providing extension work for fast finishers.

One Grammar page in each unit also features a **Game** that encourages personalized practice in a less formal context.

At the end of each Grammar page students are directed to the Student CD-ROM and the Workbook where there is further practice.

Communication

One page in every unit focuses on everyday English. Conversational language is presented in the form of a dialogue which reviews the vocabulary and grammar from the previous lessons. In a similar way to the Language focus section on page 2 of the unit, Communication lessons allow students to explore and use a new structure before they move on to more formal practice on the subsequent Grammar page.

The **You ask / You answer** feature summarizes the target language in the dialogue, while a **Pronunciation** activity draws students' attention to a specific sound, a relevant aspect of intonation, or connected speech. The students then listen to this language in different contexts before practicing it themselves in the **Pairwork** activity.

At the end of each Communication page students are directed to the Student CD-ROM and the Workbook where there is further practice.

Skills

The last two pages of the unit contain targeted skills work designed to equip students with the necessary strategies to build confidence and competence in each individual skill.

Skills lessons also provide a way of consolidating and recycling the language that students have studied throughout the unit, whilst exploring different aspects of the unit topic.

Reading texts deal with the main topic of the unit in a factual way using real-life contexts. Comprehension exercises typically start with a skimming or scanning activity, followed by more detailed questions that gradually increase in difficulty as the series progresses.

Listening activities extend the topic of the text. A variety of activity formats is used to help students develop well-rounded listening comprehension skills.

The Speaking and Writing sections give students the opportunity to respond to the unit topic with their own ideas. To help students organize their ideas, both sections usually begin with a written preparation stage. The aim is to strike a balance between giving clear, guided models on the page on the one hand, and allowing students freedom to express themselves and experiment with newly-acquired vocabulary and structures on the other.

Review Units

After every two main units there is a four-page Review unit comprising:

Grammar and Vocabulary review 2 pages

Culture club reading 1 page

My progress 1 page

The first half of each Review unit covers the main grammar and vocabulary points from the previous two units. The exercises in the **Got it?** section at the end of the second page consolidate all the grammar and vocabulary content by dealing with several language points together in each exercise. The value of this is that students can see how different areas of language behave together, rather than always seeing them in isolation.

Most teenagers are curious to know what life is like for their peers in other parts of the world. **Culture club** reading lessons give a factual account of different aspects of the English-speaking world from a young person's perspective. The **Focus on you** section at the end of the lesson invites a personal response from students in the form of a piece of writing, discussion, or oral presentation.

The **My progress** page is a self-assessment page correlated to the Common European Framework of Reference. It is very motivating for students to reflect on their progress and this type of activity is also very helpful in encouraging students to take responsibility for their own learning.

Remember

After Unit 4 there is a two-page review covering the main grammar and vocabulary points from the first half of the book. In the split edition of *Got it!*, the Remember unit opens the second volume at each level.

Curriculum extra

There are four cross-curricular reading and project lessons in the Student Book, providing two pages of material for each block of four units. The **Curriculum extra** lessons link to the themes of the corresponding Student Book units, as well as to subjects that students typically study in their own language, such as geography, science, math, art, and history.

Each lesson concludes with a project that synthesizes the language focus and the content of the cross-curricular theme and gives students the opportunity to develop their creativity. The projects can be done in class or assigned for homework. Depending on time available and the needs of the students, the projects can be done in groups, pairs, or individually.

Workbook

The Workbook section contains eight six-page units of extra practice of the language and skills taught in the Student Book. The Workbook exercises can be completed in class or for homework.

The first two pages of each Workbook unit summarize the grammar structures introduced in the corresponding Student Book unit with comprehensive charts and detailed grammar notes.

The following two pages provide extra vocabulary and grammar practice. The last two pages provide additional practice to accompany the Student Book Communication lesson, and further reading and writing practice.

Student CD-ROM

The Student CD-ROM contains interactive practice of the grammar, vocabulary, and communication sections of each unit of the Student Book.

For each Student Book unit there are eight grammar activities and two vocabulary exercises, and a communication exercise with audio. Communication exercises feature extra audio based on the corresponding Student Book dialogues.

From the vocabulary screens students can click to access a **word list** with audio to listen to the vocabulary from the corresponding Student Book unit.

There are two games for every two units. The first, in which students have to identify the odd one out, practices vocabulary; in the second game students play against an opponent and have to complete correct grammatical sentences or questions. For each game, students can choose progress up to three levels of difficulty.

In *Got it!* levels 2 and 3, the CD-ROM provides access to a free interactive online test. Level 2 links to a KET for Schools practice test, and level 3 links to a PET for Schools practice test. For more details, and to purchase further practice tests, visit **oxfordenglishtesting.com**.

Teacher's Book

The Teacher's Book contains detailed lesson notes and answers for all the Student Book and Workbook material.

Each Teacher's Book unit starts with a summary of the areas of vocabulary, grammar, communication, skills, and topical themes covered in the Student Book unit. Also listed are themes relating to values and responsible citizenship, such as:

- Ethics and morals;
- Society, including the themes of respect, solidarity, and justice;
- Multiculturalism, including anthropology, human rights, cultural studies, sociology, and historical, geographical, legal, and ethical perspectives;
- The Environment, including protecting the environment, and natural cycles;
- Work and consumerism, including mass communication, advertising, sales, workers' rights, and consumer rights;
- Health.

The notes include a description of the aim of every lesson section in the Student Book, followed by detailed instructions and answers.

There are also suggestions for Warm-up activities, and Extra activities that can be used to extend the Student Book content according to the needs and abilities of each class.

The Student Book is full of factual information and references to the real world. The teaching notes provide support for this by giving additional notes and cultural facts in the **Background information** notes.

Teenage students have an insatiable interest in music and popular culture, and the use of songs to consolidate the linguistic and topical contents of the Student Book can be an effective way of motivating students. The teaching notes for each Review unit include suggestions for suitable songs that can be exploited for this purpose. The songs have been chosen because of their lexical, grammatical, or thematic link to the corresponding units.

See page 9 for suggestions on how to exploit songs in class.

Class Audio CD

There are two Class Audio CDs which are for classroom use. Class Audio CD1 contains all the Student Book audio, while Class Audio CD2 contains audio recordings of the Skills readings and listening test audio. There is a track listing for Class Audio CD1 on page 13.

iTools

The *Got it!* iTools provides a powerful classroom resource for the teacher. In addition to a fully interactive Student Book, each iTools disc contains a wealth of extra support material.

Interactive Student Book

iTools contains the complete content of the Student Book and Workbook, designed to be projected in class. To take full advantage of its rich interactive content, it should be used with an interactive whiteboard, but may also be used with a computer connected to a screen or data projector.

In addition to the standard interactive functions common to interactive whiteboards, other features of iTools include:

- full audio content, launched directly from the Student Book page;
- audio script and answer keys displayed at the click of a button;
- full zoom functionality;
- extra interactivity on selected exercises;
- quick links from each Student Book lesson to the corresponding Workbook page.

For full details, see the separate documentation included with the iTools disc.

Extra resources

Alongside the Student Book and Workbook, there is a large amount of extra resource material included on each iTools disc. The extra resources provide support material for consolidation, extension, mixed ability classes, and assessment. All resources are printable, and can also be projected in class.

Tests

For each level of *Got it!*, there are eight unit tests and four review tests, all of which can be opened using Microsoft® Word and edited before printing.

The unit tests include vocabulary and grammar questions, dialogue work, and a writing task. Each test is scored out of 50 points.

The review tests focus on vocabulary and grammar, and reading, writing, and listening skills. Each test is scored out of 100 points.

Regular assessment makes it easier to monitor students' progress during each semester. Teachers can keep a record of individual students' progress using the Student's progress record sheet on page 12.

Grammar and vocabulary

Grammar help and Vocabulary help worksheets for each unit provide additional practice of the Student Book material at a basic level, and are ideal for giving weaker students more practice.

Grammar extension and Vocabulary extension worksheets offer more challenging practice for the more able students.

Pairwork

There is one pairwork worksheet per unit, giving oral practice of the grammar and vocabulary of the corresponding unit.

Puzzles and games

One page of puzzles is included for each unit, and two board games for each level of the series. Although these resources give practice of the main grammar and vocabulary of the unit, the emphasis is on fun activities, such as crosswords, wordsearches, and code breakers.

Video lessons

iTools contains four video documentaries per level, with accompanying worksheets. When used with an interactive whiteboard, the video clips can be launched directly from the icon on the worksheet.

Practice tests for Cambridge ESOL examinations

Levels 2 and 3 of *Got it!* iTools include a printable practice test for Cambridge ESOL examinations: a KET practice test for level 2, and a PET practice test for level 3.

Test Builder

The inclusion of a Test Builder with *Got it!* adds greater flexibility to the assessment options available to the teacher. A large database of questions in a variety of different formats allows for an almost limitless number of tests to be created, edited, and customized. Once created, tests can be printed, saved, and edited again if necessary.

The Test Builder also features listening tests. The audio for these tests is included on the same disc.

For full details, see the separate documentation included with the Test Builder disc.

DVD

Two DVDs accompany the series, with four documentaries for each level. The material deals with different cultural aspects of the English-speaking world, and is closely linked to the language syllabus and topical themes of the Student Book. The video clips are designed to be used after completion of each Review unit, or after every second main unit.

The DVD also contains printable worksheets, teaching notes, answer keys, and scripts. These can be accessed when the disc is used with a computer.

In addition to the comprehension questions on the worksheets, there are multiple-choice questions displayed on screen after each documentary. The correct answer can be selected with the remote control if viewed on a DVD player, or using a mouse if viewed on a computer.

Interactive content

Got it! offers interactive content for delivery via a Learning Management System.

The content includes extra video, featuring authentic interviews with young people from the U.S.

There is also additional audio and listening comprehension work corresponding to each main unit of the Student Book and each Review unit.

Classroom management

An English-speaking environment

- Use English for classroom instructions as often as you can, and ask students to use English as well. For example: *Open your books at page 10. Let's look at exercise 3. Raise your hand. Work in pairs. Ask your partner*, etc.
- Students should be encouraged to use expressions such as: *How do you say … in English? How do you spell …? I don't understand. Please can you repeat that? Can you say that more slowly, please? Can we listen to that again, please? Can I go to the bathroom?*

Managing large classes

Large classes are easier to manage if you establish routines such as:

- Write a plan of the day's activities on the board.
- Make sure that everyone understands the task before they start. Give clear examples and ask students to provide a few as well.
- Set time limits for all activities and remind students of them: *You have two minutes left.*
- Walk around the class, monitoring while students work.
- Get to know your students' personalities and learning styles so that you can maximize their potential in class.
- Allow stronger students to help weaker students while ensuring that there is always an atmosphere of mutual respect and understanding.

Group and pairwork

The interaction from working in small groups or in pairs is vital in a language classroom, and students quickly get used to what to expect. Here are some tips for organizing group work in large classes:

- Don't have more than five students per group.
- Set up group activities quickly by allocating students with a letter (A, B, C, etc.). Students form groups with other students who have the same letter.
- Demonstrate tasks with one pair or group.

Songs

Here are some ways in which songs can be exploited:

- **Gap-fill:** There are many variations of this type of activity, in which students are given the lyrics with certain key words deleted. To make it easier for students, the missing words can be grouped together in a box. As students read the lyrics, they try to fill in the gaps, then they listen and check. If you wish to make the activity more challenging, you could add extra words as distractors, or not provide the missing words at all. It is important to choose the gapped words carefully, however, both so that they are audible, and so that students can guess from the context which word makes most sense in each gap.
- **Correct the mistakes:** Include some incorrect words or information in the lyrics. Ask students to identify where the mistakes are and replace them with the correct words, before they listen to the song to check their answers.

- **Choose the correct alternative:** At regular points in the lyrics, students have to choose between two or more alternative words or phrases to complete the lyrics correctly. Students then listen and check.
- **Put the verses in the correct order:** This activity works especially well with songs that tell a story. Students are given the verses in the wrong order, and they have to guess the correct order before listening to the song.
- **Match rhyming words:** Many songs are structured so that alternating lines end with rhyming words, and this provides an excellent opportunity to work on different sounds. One useful activity is to give students the lyrics with the lines of each verse jumbled. Students then attempt to unjumble the lines, according to which lines rhyme with each other, before listening to the song to check their ideas. Another variation is for students to choose between two alternatives to end each line. This could mean choosing the word that provides the best rhyme, for example, or the word that makes most sense in the context.
- **Match words to definitions:** Songs often contain informal expressions, idioms, and "untidy" grammar. With stronger groups it can be useful to have students try to match difficult words and expressions to definitions or explanations. Alternatively, where lyrics feature more standard items of vocabulary, students could work together in groups to find the words in a dictionary and agree on a definition.

Feedback

It is important for students to have a sense of how they have performed. Provide feedback while you are monitoring activities. Alternatively, you can assess an exercise afterward with the whole class: students can put up their hands to indicate how many answers they shared in pairs or groups, how hard or easy the task was, etc.

Suggestions for further reading

General reference

Oxford Guide to British and American Culture – 2nd Edition

The Oxford Picture Dictionary – New edition

Practical English Usage – 3rd Edition

Grammar

The Good Grammar Book (Elementary to Lower-Intermediate) by Michael Swan and Catherine Walter

Grammar (Beginner to Pre-intermediate) New Edition by Jennifer Seidl

Grammar Sense (1–3) by Susan Kesner Bland

Graded readers

The Oxford Bookworms Library (Elementary to Pre-intermediate) – fiction and non-fiction readers that are ideal for extended reading, and cultural, and cross-curricular studies.

Ideas for supplementary activities and teacher development

Oxford Basics

Resource Books for Teachers

Common European Framework of Reference (CEFR)

The Common European Framework of Reference (CEFR) was designed to promote a consistent interpretation of foreign-language competence among the member states of the European Union. Today, the use of the CEFR has expanded beyond the boundaries of Europe, and it is used in other regions of the world, including Latin America, Asia, and the Middle East.

The CEFR defines linguistic competence in three levels: A, B, and C. Each of these levels is split into two sub-levels:

A	Basic User	A1	Breakthrough
		A2	Waystage
B	Independent User	B1	Threshold
		B2	Vantage
C	Proficient User	C1	Effectiveness
		C2	Mastery

The CEFR provides teachers with a structure for assessing their students' progress as well as monitoring specific language objectives and achievements. Students respond to the CEFR statements in the Reviews after Units 2, 4, 6, and 8.

Got it! aims to enable students to move from no English or level A1 and into level B2 at the end of the four years of the course.

Descriptions of the CEFR levels

Basic User

A1 Can understand and use familiar everyday expressions and very basic phrases aimed at the satisfaction and needs of a concrete type. Can introduce him/herself and others and can ask and answer questions about personal details such as where he/she lives, people he/she knows and things he/she has. Can interact in a simple way provided the other person talks slowly and clearly and is prepared to help.

A2 Can understand sentences and frequently used expressions related to areas of most immediate relevance (e.g. very basic personal and family information, shopping, geography, employment). Can communicate in simple and routine tasks requiring a simple and direct exchange of information on familiar and routine matters. Can describe in simple terms aspect of his/her background, immediate environment and matters in areas of immediate need.

Independent User

B1 Can understand the main points of clear standard input on familiar matters regularly encountered in work, school, leisure, etc. Can deal with most situations likely to arise whilst travelling in an area where the language is spoken. Can produce simple connected text on topics which are familiar or of personal interest. Can describe experiences and events, dreams, hopes & ambitions and briefly give reasons and explanations for opinions and plans.

B2 Can understand the main ideas of complex text on both concrete and abstract topics, including technical discussions in his/her field of specialization. Can interact with a degree of fluency and spontaneity that makes regular interaction with native speakers quite possible without strain for either party. Can produce clear, detailed text on a wide range of subjects and explain a viewpoint on a topical issue giving the advantages and disadvantages of various options.

English Portfolio

The Language Portfolio has been developed in conjunction with the CEFR. It is a folder kept by the students which details their experiences of English and learning English. A Language Portfolio consists of the following:

A language Biography

A checklist for students to assess their own language skills in terms of "What I can do". In *Got it!,* these are found in the Review Units after Units 2, 4, 6, and 8.

Tools to help students identify their learning style and objectives. See the photocopiable form for students on page 11.

A checklist of learning activities outside the classroom. See the photocopiable form for students on page 12.

A language Passport

An overview of the level attained by the student in English at the end of the year.

A Dossier

Samples of the student's work, including tests, written work, projects, or other student-generated materials. In order to assist students in compilation of a Language Portfolio, you may ask them to record their answers to the CEF checklist on a separate sheet of paper and keep it in a folder. In addition, provide each student with a copy of the photocopiable form from page 11 once they have completed the CEFR checklist in the book. Ask them to keep these forms in their portfolio folder as well. Finally, encourage students to choose several pieces of their work from different points in the year to compile the dossier of their portfolio.

Student self-assessment checklist

What I remember:

Useful grammar:

_____

_____

_____

Useful vocabulary:

_____

_____

_____

Objectives:

One thing I need to improve:

_____

_____

_____

How can I improve this?

_____

What did you do in English outside class?

____ Do homework

____ Learn new words

____ Revise before a test

____ Listen to music

____ Read something extra in English

____ Watch a TV show, video, or DVD

____ Write an e-mail or chat

____ Look at web pages

____ Speak to someone in English

____ Read a magazine

____ Other activities: _____

Student's progress record sheet

Name _____

Class / Grade _____

	Date	Classwork: continuous assessment			Test results
		Grammar	Vocabulary	Skills	
Unit 1					
Unit 2					
Unit 3					
Unit 4					
Unit 5					
Unit 6					
Unit 7					
Unit 8					

	Comments
Units 1–2	
Units 3–4	
Units 5–6	
Units 7–8	

Class Audio CD1 track list

Contents

Track	Contents		Track	Contents
1.1	Title		**1.33**	Unit 4, Page 42, Exercise 2
1.2	Unit 1, Page 10, Exercise 1		**1.34**	Unit 4, Page 42, Exercise 3
1.3	Unit 1, Page 11, Exercise 4		**1.35**	Unit 4, Page 45, Exercise 3
1.4	Unit 1, Page 12, Exercise 1		**1.36**	Unit 5, Page 52, Exercise 1
1.5	Unit 1, Page 12, Exercise 2		**1.37**	Unit 5, Page 53, Exercise 4
1.6	Unit 1, Page 14, Exercise 1		**1.38**	Unit 5, Page 54, Exercise 2
1.7	Unit 1, Page 14, Exercise 2		**1.39**	Unit 5, Page 56, Exercise 1
1.8	Unit 1, Page 14, Exercise 3		**1.40**	Unit 5, Page 56, Exercise 2
1.9	Unit 1, Page 17, Exercise 2		**1.41**	Unit 5, Page 56, Exercise 3
1.10	Unit 2, Page 18, Exercise 1		**1.42**	Unit 5, Page 59, Exercise 2
1.11	Unit 2, Page 19, Exercise 4		**1.43**	Unit 6, Page 60, Exercise 1
1.12	Unit 2, Page 20, Exercise 1		**1.44**	Unit 6, Page 61, Exercise 4
1.13	Unit 2, Page 20, Exercise 2		**1.45**	Unit 6, Page 62, Exercise 2
1.14	Unit 2, Page 22, Exercise 1		**1.46**	Unit 6, Page 64, Exercise 1
1.15	Unit 2, Page 22, Exercise 2		**1.47**	Unit 6, Page 64, Exercise 2
1.16	Unit 2, Page 22, Exercise 3		**1.48**	Unit 6, Page 64, Exercise 3
1.17	Unit 2, Page 25, Exercise 2		**1.49**	Unit 6, Page 67, Exercise 3
1.18	Unit 3, Page 30, Exercise 1		**1.50**	Unit 7, Page 72, Exercise 1
1.19	Unit 3, Page 31, Exercise 4		**1.51**	Unit 7, Page 73, Exercise 4
1.20	Unit 3, Page 32, Exercise 1		**1.52**	Unit 7, Page 74, Exercise 2
1.21	Unit 3, Page 33, Exercise 3		**1.53**	Unit 7, Page 76, Exercise 1
1.22	Unit 3, Page 33, Exercise 4		**1.54**	Unit 7, Page 76, Exercise 2
1.23	Unit 3, Page 34, Exercise 1		**1.55**	Unit 7, Page 76, Exercise 3
1.24	Unit 3, Page 34, Exercise 2		**1.56**	Unit 7, Page 76, Exercise 4
1.25	Unit 3, Page 34, Exercise 3		**1.57**	Unit 7, Page 79, Exercise 2
1.26	Unit 3, Page 34, Exercise 4		**1.58**	Unit 8, Page 80, Exercise 1
1.27	Unit 3, Page 37, Exercise 2		**1.59**	Unit 8, Page 81, Exercise 4
1.28	Unit 4, Page 38, Exercise 1		**1.60**	Unit 8, Page 82, Exercise 1
1.29	Unit 4, Page 39, Exercise 4		**1.61**	Unit 8, Page 84, Exercise 1
1.30	Unit 4, Page 40, Exercise 2		**1.62**	Unit 8, Page 84, Exercise 2
1.31	Unit 4, Page 40, Exercise 3		**1.63**	Unit 8, Page 84, Exercise 3
1.32	Unit 4, Page 42, Exercise 1		**1.64**	Unit 8, Page 87, Exercise 3

Contents

Making requests **Pronunciation:** Rising intonation in questions and falling intonation in answers	**Reading:** A magazine article about basketball coaches **Listening:** A phone call about a summer camp **Speaking:** A conversation a summer camp **Writing:** A postcard about a summer camp
Agreeing and disagreeing **Pronunciation:** Sentence stress	**Reading:** A biography of Bono **Listening:** A biography of Elvis Presley **Speaking:** Factfiles of Justin Timberlake and Shakira **Writing:** A personal profile of your favorite pop singer

Curriculum extra A, Music: pages C1–C2

Apologizing and making excuses **Pronunciation:** /ɑ/ and /oʊ/	**Reading:** A biography of Christopher Columbus **Listening:** A biography of George Washington **Speaking:** A presentation of the life of William Shakespeare or Marie Curie **Writing:** An description of the life of William Shakespeare or Marie Curie
Buying a movie ticket **Pronunciation:** /s/, /k/, and /tʃ/	**Reading:** An interview with Shia LaBeouf **Listening:** A conversation about a movie **Speaking:** Discussing a movie **Writing:** A description of two movies

Curriculum extra B, Media studies: pages C3–C4

Making arrangements **Pronunciation:** /oʊ/ and /u/	**Reading:** A magazine article about skateboarding across Australia **Listening:** An interview with a skateboarder **Speaking:** A trip to San Diego **Writing:** An e-mail about a trip
Ordering food and drink **Pronunciation:** *would you*	**Reading:** A magazine article about a teen celebrity chef **Listening:** Two teenagers talking about their diets **Speaking:** A food survey **Writing:** Your diet

Curriculum extra C, Citizenship: pages C5–C6

Asking for tourist information **Pronunciation:** /ə/	**Reading:** A magazine article about bizarre pets **Listening:** Giving advice about guinea pigs and hamsters **Speaking:** Talking about your favorite animals **Writing:** The differences between traditional and exotic pets
Making a phone call **Pronunciation:** /h/	**Reading:** A magazine article about colors **Listening:** Teenagers talking about their favorite colors **Speaking:** Talking about your favorite colors **Writing:** A text about your favorite colors

Curriculum extra D, Geography: pages C7–C8

Welcome

Grammar
be: Simple present
Demonstratives: *this, that, these, those*
There is (There's) / There are
Simple present
Adverbs of frequency
How often …?
can (ability)
Imperatives
Present progressive

Vocabulary
Countries and nationalities
Family
Daily routines and free-time activities
House and furniture
Sports
Clothes

Vocabulary

Countries and nationalities   PAGE 4

Aim

To review countries and nationalities

Warm-up

- Call out one or two countries and nationalities from the list and ask students to give you the nationality and country.

Exercise 1

- Students match the countries with the flags. Then they write the nationalities.
- Students can check answers in pairs.
- Check the answers with the class.

ANSWERS
1 the United Kingdom; British   2 Canada; Canadian
3 Japan; Japanese   4 the United States; American
5 South Korea; South Korean

Family   PAGE 4

Aim

To review family vocabulary

Warm-up

- Ask students the names of one or two people in their family, e.g. *What's your mom's name?, What's your grandpa's name?*

Exercise 2

- Students look at Ella's family tree and complete the sentences.
- Students can check answers in pairs.
- Check the answers with the class. You can draw Ella's family tree on the board and ask volunteers to come out and write the answers.

ANSWERS
1 sister   2 mom   3 grandma   4 cousin   5 brother
6 dad   7 sister   8 aunt   9 uncle   10 grandparents

Daily routines and free-time activities   PAGE 4

Aim

To review daily routines and free-time activities

Warm-up

- Ask students what time they get up in the morning and what they have for breakfast.

Exercise 3

- Students complete the text individually or in pairs.
- Remind them to think about the correct verb form to use.
- Check the answers with the class.

ANSWERS
1 go shopping   2 have lunch   3 watch TV
4 play computer games   5 go to the movies   6 go to bed

House and furniture   PAGE 5

Aim

To review house and furniture vocabulary

Warm-up

- Books closed. Ask students how many rooms in a house they can remember. Write them on the board.

Exercise 4

- In pairs, students look at the picture and write the names of the rooms (A–E). They then write the names of the furniture in each room (1–8).
- Remind them they can refer to the list of rooms on the board from the *Warm-up* if necessary.
- Check the answers with the class.

ANSWERS
B bathroom   C kitchen   D dining room   E living room
2 sink   3 shower   4 stove   5 refrigerator   6 table
7 sofa   8 armchair

Sports PAGE 5

Aim

To review sports vocabulary

Warm-up

- Ask students: *Do you play any sports? If so, which ones?* Write any sports students play on the board.

Exercise 5

- Students look at the pictures and complete the crossword. They then find the mystery sport.
- Check the answers with the class.

ANSWERS

1 basketball   2 baseball   3 soccer   4 karate
5 gymnastics   6 swimming   7 cycling
Mystery sport: track and field

Clothes PAGE 5

Aim

To review clothes vocabulary

Warm-up

- Ask students to describe what you are wearing today.

Exercise 6

- Students look at the pictures and label the clothes.
- Check the answers with the class.

ANSWERS

1 top   2 jacket   3 skirt   4 shoes   5 cap   6 sweatshirt
7 pants   8 sneakers

Exercise 7

- Individually, students write a sentence describing what they are wearing.

ANSWERS

Students' own answers.

Grammar

be: Simple present PAGE 6

Aim

To review *be*, simple present: all forms

Warm-up

- Write the names of famous stars on the board. Students ask and answer questions about the stars, e.g. SS1: *What's his name?* SS2: *His name's Johnny Depp.*

Exercise 1

- Students read the factfile and complete the sentences. Remind them to think about which form of *be* they need.
- Check the answers with the class.

ANSWERS

1 is   2 isn't   3 are   4 isn't   5 aren't   6 are

Exercise 2

- Students read the information. Then they write the questions and answer them.
- Monitor and check that students are using the correct forms of *be* simple present and review if necessary.

ANSWERS

What's your name?   1 How old are you?   2 Are you from Brazil?
3 Is music your favorite subject?   4 Who are your friends?
5 Is Green Day your favorite band?
Students' own answers.

Demonstratives: *this, that, these, those* PAGE 6

Aim

To review demonstratives *this, that, these, those*

Warm-up

- Point to or hold up classroom objects and elicit the appropriate demonstrative from students. For example, point to a pen on your desk and encourage students to say *this.*

Exercise 3

- Students complete the sentences with the demonstratives.
- They can compare answers in pairs.
- Check the answers with the class.

ANSWERS

1 These   2 This   3 That   4 Those

There is (There's) / There are PAGE 6

Aim

To review *there is / there are* affirmative and negative

Warm-up

- Books closed. Read the first sentence from the text in exercise 4 and elicit the correct answer (*there is*).

Exercise 4

- Students look at the pictures and complete the text.
- Monitor and check that they are using the correct form of *there is / are*.
- Students can compare answers in pairs.
- Check the answers with the class.

ANSWERS

1 there is   2 There isn't   3 there is   4 there are   5 There
isn't   6 there is   7 There are   8 There aren't   9 there is

Simple present PAGE 7

Aim

To review the simple present: all forms

Warm-up

- Ask students one or two questions, e.g. *What time do you get up?* and elicit simple present answers.

Exercise 5

- Students write questions and answer them.
- Monitor and check that students are using the simple present correctly and review if necessary.
- Students can compare answers in pairs.
- Check the answers with the class. You can ask volunteers to read out their answers.

ANSWERS

1 Does Jenny have breakfast in the kitchen?
  No, she doesn't. / She doesn't have breakfast in the kitchen.
  She has breakfast in the living room.
2 Do Larry and Walter play baseball?
  No, they don't. / They don't play baseball.
  They play basketball.
3 Does Ethan play the guitar?
  No, he doesn't. / He doesn't play the guitar.
  He plays the piano.
4 Do Tom and Laura live in a small house?
  No, they don't. / They don't live in a small house.
  They live in a big house.
5 Does the show start at 8 o'clock?
  No, it doesn't. / It doesn't start at 8 o'clock.
  It starts at 8:30.

Exercise 6

- Students read the e-mail and complete it with the correct simple present form of the verbs.
- Monitor and check that they are using the correct forms and make a note of any repeated errors to go over at the end of the lesson.
- Check the answers with the class.

ANSWERS

1 go 2 get up 3 have 4 teaches 5 starts 6 finishes
7 get 8 watch 9 do 10 gets 11 have 12 don't go
13 listen 14 chat 15 go 16 do you go 17 do you do

Exercise 7

- Students write questions about Melissa and then answer them using the e-mail in exercise 6.
- Elicit or remind students how to form *Wh-* questions with the simple present if necessary.
- Check the answers with the class.

ANSWERS

1 Where does she go to school?
  She goes to school at Hamilton Junior High School.
2 Who does she have breakfast with?
  She has breakfast with her family.
3 What does her mom teach? She teaches P.E.
4 What time does school start? It starts at 8:45 a.m.
5 What does she do before dinner?
  She watches TV and she does her homework.
6 What do Melissa and her friends do after dinner?
  They chat on the Internet.

Adverbs of frequency PAGE 7

Aim

To review adverbs of frequency

Warm-up

- Ask students one or two questions about their daily routines to elicit adverbs of frequency e.g. T: *What do you do after school?* SS: *I always watch TV / do my homework*, etc.

Exercise 8

- Students put the adverbs into the correct order.
- Encourage them to look at the symbols to help them.
- Check the answers with the class. You can copy the diagram onto the board and ask volunteers to come out and write the answers on the board.

ANSWERS

1 usually 2 often 3 sometimes 4 rarely

Exercise 9

- Students rewrite the sentences with the adverbs of frequency in the correct place.
- Remind them to refer back to their answers in exercise 8 if necessary.
- Check the answers with the class.

ANSWERS

1 Paula always takes a shower before breakfast.
2 Our teacher is never late for class.
3 Ken often gets up at 8 a.m.
4 They rarely go to bed before 10 p.m.
5 I usually go cycling with my dad.
6 He's often happy.

How often …? PAGE 8

Aim

To review *How often …?* questions and answers

Warm-up

- Ask students one or two questions using *How often …?* and elicit answers, e.g. *How often do you watch TV?*

Exercise 10

- Students look at Helen's schedule and write questions about how often she does things.
- Monitor and check that students are using the correct questions and answer forms, and time expressions.
- Check the answers with the class.

ANSWERS

1 How often does she watch TV?
  She watches TV four times a week.
2 How often does she go to the sports center with Kelly?
  She goes to the sports center with Kelly three times a week.
3 How often does she have pizza with her friends?
  She has pizza with her friends once a week.
4 How often does she visit her grandma?
  She visits her grandma twice a week.
5 How often does she go shopping with her mom?
  She goes shopping with her mom one a week.

can (ability) `PAGE 8`

Aim

To review *can* (for ability): all forms

Warm-up

- Ask students one or two questions about what they can / can't do, e.g. *Ana, can you play the guitar?*

Exercise 11

- Students look at the pictures and write questions and answers about what the people can / can't do.
- Monitor and check that students are using *can* correctly and review as necessary.
- Check the answers with the class.

`ANSWERS`

1 Can Robbie play cards?
  Yes, he can. He can play cards, but he can't play chess.
2 Can the children swim?
  Yes, they can. They can swim, but they can't ride a bike.
3 Can Olivia play the guitar?
  Yes, she can. She can play the guitar, but she can't play the piano.
4 Can Mark ski?
  Yes, he can. He can ski, but he can't play tennis.
5 Can my little brother read?
  Yes, he can. He can read, but he can't write.

Imperatives `PAGE 8`

Aim

To review affirmative and negative imperative forms

Warm-up

- Call out one or two affirmative imperatives and ask students to make them negative, e.g. T: *Stand up!* SS: *Don't stand up!*

Exercise 12

- Students read and complete the school rules with the correct imperative forms.
- They can compare answers in pairs.
- Check the answers with the class.

`ANSWERS`

3 Don't use   4 Don't eat   5 Stand up   6 Walk
7 Don't leave

Present progressive `PAGE 9`

Aim

To review present progressive affirmative, negative, interrogative, and short answers

Warm-up

- Ask one or two present progressive questions to elicit affirmative forms from students, e.g. *What are you wearing today, Jõao?*

Exercise 13

- Give students a few minutes to look at the picture and decide what the teenagers (1–5) are doing.
- Ask for volunteers to give you the answers. Monitor for correct use of present progressive affirmative and do a quick review if necessary.

`ANSWERS`

2 They're playing computer games.
3 She's singing.
4 They're dancing.
5 They're chatting. / They're talking.

Exercise 14

- Students read the sentences and correct the mistakes about teenagers 6–10. Remind them to look carefully at the picture.
- Students can compare answers in pairs.
- Check the answers with the class.

`ANSWERS`

7 He isn't doing homework. He's eating a hot dog.
8 He isn't writing an e-mail. He's reading a magazine.
9 She isn't dancing. She's talking on her cell phone. / She's using a cell phone.
10 She isn't playing chess. She's drinking. / She's having a drink.

Exercise 15

- Students write questions about the picture and then answer them.
- They can compare answers in pairs.
- Check the answers with the class.

`ANSWERS`

1 What is the girl with the camera wearing?
  She's wearing a dress.
2 What is the dog doing?
  It's sleeping under the table.
3 Where is the cat sitting?
  It's sitting on the (back of the) sofa.
4 How many people are standing up?
  Six people are standing up.
5 How many people are sitting down?
  Eight people are sitting down.

Exercise 16

- Students read and complete the dialogue with the correct present progressive form of the verbs.
- Students can compare answers in pairs.
- Check the answers with the class.

`ANSWERS`

1 are you doing   2 'm watching   3 're having   4 's trying
5 isn't singing   6 's shouting   7 are they doing
8 're playing   9 's winning   10 'm not watching

1 Sam's playing today

Grammar
Simple present / Present progressive
Possessive pronouns
Adverbs of manner: Regular and irregular

Vocabulary
Physical descriptions

Communication
Making requests

Skills
Reading: A text about basketball stars
Listening: Two friends talking on the phone
Speaking: A phone conversation with a friend
Writing: A postcard to a friend

Topics
Sport: Health and fitness
Multiculturalism: Summer camps

Presentation PAGE 10

Aim
To present the new language in a motivating context

Story
Zoe is writing an article about the school basketball team for the school yearbook. She is interviewing Coach Carson while the team is playing a game. The star player is Sam, but he isn't playing well today. Zoe tries to interview Sam after the game, but he is interrupted by a phone call from his mom.

Warm-up
- Ask students to look at the photo. Ask: *Who can you see in the photo?* (three boys, a girl, and a teacher) *Where are they?* (in the school gym) *What are the three boys doing?* (they're playing basketball).

Exercise 1 Read and listen 1.2
- Read through the three names with the class.
- Play the CD. Students listen and read and find the answer.
- Check the answer with the class.
- Go through the *Check it out!* box and the dialogue. Make sure that students understand the meaning of the phrases.
- Play the CD again. Students listen and repeat chorally, then individually.

Transcript STUDENT BOOK PAGE 10

ANSWER
c Sam

Exercise 2 Comprehension
- Students read the dialogue again and answer the questions.
- Check the answers with the class.

ANSWERS
1 Sam is the basketball team's star player.
2 Teo is in Zoe's class.
3 He practices basketball every day.
4 Sam's mom calls him after the game.

Extra activity
- In groups of four, students can act out the dialogue.

Consolidation
- Remind students to copy any new vocabulary from the dialogue into their vocabulary books.

Language focus PAGE 11

Aim
To practice the target language in a new context

Exercise 3 Dialogue focus
- Students read the mini-dialogues and complete them with the questions from the box.
- Remind them to look back at exercise 1 if necessary.
- Do not check the answers at this point.

Exercise 4 1.3
- Play the CD. Students listen and check their answers.
- Students listen again and repeat chorally, then individually.

ANSWERS / AUDIO CD TRACK 1.3
1 **Zoe** I'm writing an article about the basketball team for the school yearbook. Can I ask you some questions?
  CC Yes, you can, but quickly! I'm watching the game.
  Zoe ¹Who's Sam?
  CC He's the tall boy with blond, wavy hair.
  Zoe Oh, there's Teo! He's in my class. ²Is he playing well?
  CC No, he isn't. He usually plays well, but he's playing badly today.
2 **Zoe** ³How often do you practice?
  Sam I practice every day. There's a big game in December.
3 **Zoe** ⁴Whose phone is ringing? Is it yours?
  Sam Yes, it's mine.

Exercise 5 Focus on you
- Students read the example dialogue and then write their own using the verbs in the box.
- Remind them to look back at exercise 3 if necessary.

ANSWERS
Students' own answers.

Exercise 6 Pairwork
- In pairs, students practice their dialogues from exercise 5.

Vocabulary PAGE 12

Physical descriptions

Aim

To present and practice vocabulary for physical descriptions: *black, blond, blue, brown, green, red; curly, long, short, shoulder-length, spiky, straight, wavy; short, tall; heavy, slim; beard, freckles, glasses, mustache*

Background notes

- Taylor Swift is an American country-pop singer from Wyomissing, Pennsylvania. She was born in 1989 and has been described as one of pop's finest songwriters. Her album *Fearless* won a Grammy award for album of the year in 2010.

- Felipe Massa is a Brazilian Formula 1 driver. He was born in 1981 in São Paulo. He has raced for Sauber and Ferrari. In 2009, he was seriously injured while qualifying for the Hungarian Grand Prix, but made a full recovery.

- Jack Black, whose real name is Thomas Jacob Black, is an American actor, comedian, and musician. He was born in 1969 in Santa Monica, California. He is best known for his roles in the movies *School of Rock*, *Tropic Thunder*, *Be Kind Rewind*, and as the voice of the panda Po in the animated movie *Kung Fu Panda*.

Warm-up

- Draw some simple illustrations on the board and elicit as many vocabulary items for physical descriptions as you can, e.g. *tall, short curly, straight*, etc.

- Alternatively, stronger students can describe other students in the class using physical description vocabulary they know.

Exercise 1 🎧 1.4

- Students look at the pictures, read the descriptions and match them.
- Students can compare answers in pairs.
- Play the CD. Students listen and check.

Transcript STUDENT BOOK PAGE 12

ANSWERS
1 c 2 d 3 b 4 a

Extra activity
- In pairs, students read two descriptions to their partner who guesses who it is. The partner who is guessing has their book closed.

Exercise 2 🎧 1.5

- Go through the *Look!* box with the class, drawing students' attention to the order of adjectives in English.
- Students read and complete the descriptions of the famous people.
- Monitor and check that they are using the correct adjectives in the correct order. Make a note of any repeated errors to go over at the end of the lesson.
- Students can compare answers in pairs.
- Play the CD. Students listen and check their answers.

ANSWERS / AUDIO CD TRACK 1.5
1 Taylor Swift is tall and ¹<u>slim</u>. She has ²<u>long</u>, blond, ³<u>wavy</u> hair, and blue ⁴<u>eyes</u>.
2 Felipe Massa is quite ¹<u>short</u> and ²<u>slim</u>. He has ³<u>short</u>, black hair, and ⁴<u>brown</u> eyes.

Exercise 3 Pairwork

- In pairs, students describe their favorite actor, singer, or sports personality to their partner.
- Monitor and check that students are taking turns to ask and answer questions. Make sure they are using the correct adjective order, and make a note of any repeated errors to go over at the end of the lesson.
- Ask one or two pairs to tell the class about their favorite actors, etc.

ANSWERS
Students' own answers.

Extra activity
- In pairs, students think of other famous people. They take turns to describe them to their partner who guesses who it is.
- Alternatively, you can bring in photos of famous people from magazines and give them out to students to describe to a partner.

Consolidation
- Remind students to make a note of any new vocabulary from the lesson and the information from the *Look!* box. Encourage them to record the vocabulary in a way that is useful for them, e.g. illustrations and translations, mind maps.

CD-ROM WORKBOOK PAGE W4

Grammar <small>PAGE 13</small>

Simple present / Present progressive

Aim

To present and practice the simple present / present progressive contrast

Warm-up

- Ask students what they do after school every day, and ask them what they are doing now, to elicit examples of both tenses.

Think! box

- Go through the *Think!* box with the class. Students choose the correct word in each rule.
- Remind students of the forms for each tense and the spelling rules for the simple present on page W2.

ANSWERS
1 habits
2 actions in progress now

Rules <small>PAGE W2</small>

Exercise 1

- Students read the sentences and underline the verbs.
- Students can compare answers in pairs.
- Check the answers with the class.
- You can write the sentences on the board and ask volunteers to come and underline the verbs on the board.

ANSWERS
1 Do … study   2 isn't listening   3 plays   4 'm writing
5 watch   6 doesn't play

> **Extra activity**
> - Ask students to say if the verbs they underlined in exercise 1 are simple present or present progressive. This can be done as a whole class activity.
> - If you wrote the sentences on the board in exercise 1, ask students to come out and write the verb tense on the board.
>
> **ANSWERS**
> 1 SP   2 PP   3 SP   4 PP   5 SP   6 SP

Exercise 2

- Students look at the sentences in exercise 1 again and circle the time expressions.
- Check the answers with the class.

ANSWERS
Simple present: 1 every day   3 once a week   5 always
6 very often
Present progressive: 2 at the moment   4 right now

Exercise 3

- Students read the sentences and choose the correct verbs.
- Remind them to look carefully at the time expressions before they choose the verb.
- Check the answers with the class.

ANSWERS
1 're listening   2 go   3 don't walk   4 are you doing
5 does she play   6 's watchng   7 doesn't teach

> **Extra activity 1**
> - If students need more help with exercise 3, encourage them to underline the time expressions in each item before they choose the verb.

> **Extra activity 2**
> - Call out a time expression from exercise 1 or 2 and ask students to tell you which tense should be used with it, e.g. T: *once a week* SS: *simple present*.

Exercise 4

- Students complete the sentences with the simple present or present progressive form of the verbs.
- Encourage them to read the whole text through and to look at the time expressions before they complete them.
- Students can compare answers in pairs.
- Check the answers with the class.

ANSWERS
1 1 go   2 aren't studying   3 're playing
2 1 plays   2 isn't working   3 's cooking
3 1 work   2 'm not working   3 'm visiting

> **Extra activity**
> - Students choose one of the texts in exercise 4 and write two more sentences (one simple present and one present progressive) for each text. This can be done in class or for homework.

Exercise 5 Game!

- In pairs, Student A chooses a time expression from the box and Student B makes a correct sentence, using the time expression.
- Remind them to think about the time expression they chose and to use the simple present or the present progressive.
- Monitor and make a note of any repeated errors to go over at the end of the lesson.

ANSWERS
Students' own answers.

Finished?

- Students write more sentences using the time expressions from exercise 5.
- Students can swap sentences with a partner who corrects them.
- Ask one or two pairs to read their sentences out to the class.

ANSWERS
Students' own answers.

> **Consolidation**
> - Encourage students to make a note of the rules and the time expressions, and to write examples of each tense in their grammar books. Encourage them to make notes in a way that will help them remember the form and rules easily.

CD-ROM <small>WORKBOOK PAGE W4</small>

Communication PAGE 14

Making requests

Aim

To present and practice making requests

Warm-up

- Ask a student if you can borrow their dictionary using the request they will learn in this lesson, e.g. *Carlo, can I borrow your dictionary, please?* and elicit one of the answers if possible, e.g. *Yes, OK.*

Exercise 1 🄯 1.6

- Give students a few minutes to read through the dialogues and to look at the pictures.
- Play the CD. Students listen and match the dialogues with the pictures.
- Students can compare answers in pairs.
- Check the answers with the class.
- Play the CD. Students listen again and repeat.

Transcript STUDENT BOOK PAGE 14

ANSWERS
1 b 2 c 3 a

- Go through the *You ask, You answer* box with the class, making sure that students are aware of the appropriate questions and answers for making requests.
- Ask students to look at the dialogue again and find examples of the expressions.
- In pairs, students can practice making requests using the information in the box.
- Encourage stronger students to change the words in parentheses in the box and to use their own ideas.

Extra activity

- Books closed. Give students two minutes to write down as many expressions as they can remember.
- The student with the most correct expressions is the winner.

Exercise 2 Pronunciation 🄯 1.7

- Students read through the sentences.
- Play the CD. Students listen and repeat chorally, then individually.
- Monitor and check that students are using correct intonation. If necessary, indicate with your hands when the intonation rises in the questions and falls in the reply.

Transcript STUDENT BOOK PAGE 14

Extra activity

- If students need extra practice with intonation, read the sentences from the box starting at the end. Students repeat chorally then individually, e.g. *please?, window, please?, the window, please?, open the window, please?, I open the window, please?, Can I open the window, please?*

Exercise 3 🄯 1.8

- Play the CD. Students listen and complete the requests.
- Play the CD again if necessary.
- Students can compare answers in pairs.
- Check the answers with the class.

ANSWERS / AUDIO CD TRACK 1.8

1	**Boy**	Can I have some water, please? I'm really thirsty!
	Woman	Yes, you can. There's some water in the refrigerator.
2	**Girl**	Can I use your cell phone? I don't have mine.
	Boy	No, you can't. I don't have any credit.
3	**Man**	Can I watch the news, please?
	Woman	Um … Not now. I'm watching a movie.

1 Can I have some water, please? ✓
2 Can I use your cell phone? ✗
3 Can I watch the news, please? ✗

Exercise 4 Pairwork

- In pairs, students make requests with the verbs in the box. Their partner accepts or rejects the requests.
- Monitor and check that students are asking and answering correctly. Make a note of any repeated errors to go over at the end of the lesson.

ANSWERS
Students' own answers.

Extra activity

- Ask pairs of students to act out their dialogues from exercise 4 in front of the class.

Consolidation

- Encourage students to make a note of the new language from this lesson in their vocabulary books. Remind them to write translations or examples of their own if it will help them to remember the new language more easily.

CD-ROM WORKBOOK PAGE W6

Grammar PAGE 15

Possessive pronouns

Aim

To present and practice possessive pronouns

Warm-up

- Hold up one of your belongings and say: *It's my cell phone. It's mine.* Hold up one or two of the students' belongings and elicit some more possessive pronouns.

Grammar chart / Think! box

- Go through the grammar chart with the class.
- Draw students' attention to the difference between possessive adjectives and possessive pronouns and give one or two examples to elicit some of the rules, e.g. *This is Ana's pen. It's her pen.*
- Ask students to look back at the dialogue on page 10 and find examples of possessive pronouns.
- Student read the *Think!* box and decide if the rules are true or false.
- Check the answers with the class before students look at the rules on page W3.

ANSWERS
1 True   2 False   3 True

Rules PAGE W3

Exercise 1

- Students complete the sentences with the correct possessive pronouns.
- Remind them to refer back to the grammar chart and rules if necessary.
- Students can compare answers in pairs.
- Check the answers with the class.

ANSWERS
1 yours   2 his   3 hers   4 ours   5 Theirs   6 yours

Exercise 2

- Students choose the correct answers. Remind them to refer back to the grammar chart and the rules if necessary.
- Check the answers with the class.

ANSWERS
1 mine   2 their   3 hers   4 ours   5 your; Mine

Extra activity 1

- If students need more practice with possessive pronouns, read the sentences in exercise 1 again for students to give you the correct possessive pronoun.

Extra activity 2

- Students write their own "choose the correct answers exercise" with possessive adjectives and pronouns.
- They swap with a partner who chooses the correct answers.

Adverbs of manner

Aim

To present and practice adverbs of manner

Grammar chart / Think! box

- Go through the grammar charts with the class. Elicit or explain when we use adverbs of manner *(to talk about how we do something)* and see if students can work out any more rules for adverbs of manner.
- Draw their attention to the form and spelling changes and the irregular adverbs.
- Ask them to look back at the dialogue on page 10 to find examples of adverbs of manner.
- Students read and complete the *Think!* box with the correct alternative in the rule.
- Check the answer with the class. Refer students to the rules on page W3 as necessary.

ANSWER
after

Rules PAGE W3

Exercise 3

- Students rewrite the sentences with adverbs of manner.
- Remind them to refer back to the grammar charts if necessary.
- Monitor and check that students are using adverbs correctly and make a note of any repeated errors to go over with the class at the end of the lesson.
- Check the answers with the class.

ANSWERS
1 slowly   2 beautifully   3 badly   4 fast   5 well

Extra activity

- If students need more practice with adverbs, call out an adjective for students to give you the adverb, e.g. T: *bad* SS: *badly*.

Finished?

- Students write true sentences about themselves or their family with the adverbs in the box.
- Students can swap sentences with a partner to correct.
- Ask one or two pairs to read out their sentences to the class.

ANSWERS
Students' own answers.

Consolidation

- Remind students to make a note of the grammar rules and the examples from the lesson in their grammar books. Remind them to make a note of the grammar in a way that will help them to remember it, e.g. with examples of their own.

CD-ROM   **WORKBOOK PAGE W5**

Skills PAGES 16–17

Reading

Aim

To read and understand a magazine article about basketball stars

Background note

- Pennsylvania is a state in the north east of the U.S. The state capital is Harrisburg and the largest city is Philadelphia.

Warm-up

- Ask students to look at the bottom right photo and ask one or two questions, e.g. *Who can you see?* (Two basketball players) *Where do you think they are?*
- Ask students to read the text quickly and to find the name of the basketball team Corey and Greg play for (the *Pittsburgh Players*).

Exercise 1

- Remind students to read the sentences carefully first and to look for the relevant information in the text. Remind them too that they do not need to understand every word. They should use the context to help them guess meaning where possible.
- Students read the text individually and correct the mistakes in the sentences.
- Check the answers with the class.

ANSWERS

1 Corey and Greg play for a professional <u>basketball</u> team.
2 They practice <u>every morning</u>.
3 This week, <u>they're doing something different</u> / <u>they're coaching teenagers on a summer basketball camp</u>.
4 The *Pittsburgh Players Basketball Camp* is for young <u>teenagers</u>.
5 <u>Some of the teenagers</u> can play basketball well, <u>but others can't play at all</u>.
6 The name of Laura's team is <u>*The Red Dragons*</u>.
7 <u>Four of Laura's friends from school</u> are in her team.
8 Laura's team is <u>doing well</u> in the championship at the moment.

Extra activity

- Give students a few minutes to read the text again and memorize as much as they can.
- Books closed. Ask students some more comprehension questions, e.g. *How tall is Corey?* (2.10 m) *How tall is Greg?* (2.12 m) *Where do they usually play basketball?* (Pennsylvania), etc.

Listening

Aim

To listen to a phone conversation between two friends

Background notes

- Elkridge is in the state of Maryland in the U.S. It is very small with a population estimated at less than 25,000.

- Baltimore is in Maryland. It is a major U.S. seaport and has a population of about 636,000.

Warm-up

- Ask students: *What kind of things do you think you might hear Bruno and Christian talk about?*
- Stronger students can read and predict the answers before they listen.

Exercise 2 🎵 1.9

- Give students time to read the answer choices before they listen.
- Play the CD. Students listen and choose the correct answers.
- Remind them that they do not need to understand every word, but they should focus on the key information in the answer choices.
- Check the answers with the class.

ANSWERS / AUDIO CD TRACK 1.9

Bruno	Hello.
Christian	Hi Bruno. It's Christian. How are things?
Bruno	Oh, hi Christian! I'm cool, thanks.
Christian	Hey! Where <u>are you</u>?
Bruno	I'm in a place called Elkridge. It's near Baltimore. I'm staying at a summer camp here.
Christian	Wow! [1]What type of <u>camp</u> is it?
Bruno	It's a theater camp. You know, drama, music, and dance.
Christian	Really? [2]What's <u>it</u> like?
Bruno	It's fantastic!
Christian	[3]What <u>are you</u> doing at the camp?
Bruno	A drama course.
Christian	Oh, yeah? Is your sister, Rosa, there too?
Bruno	Yeah, she is, but she's doing dance.
Christian	[4]Do you <u>do</u> the course all day?
Bruno	No, we don't. We always act in the mornings, but we do different activities in the afternoons and evenings.
Christian	[5]What other <u>activities</u> are there?
Bruno	Well, we usually play sports in the afternoon. You can play soccer and tennis or go swimming. I usually play soccer. Then, in the evenings we watch movies or have a party.
Christian	[6]<u>What's</u> your favorite activity?
Bruno	The drama course. It's awesome! Oh, Christian! It's dinner time.
Christian	No problem. See you!
Bruno	Bye! Thanks for calling.

1 b   2 a   3 b   4 b   5 a   6 a

Exercise 3 🎵 1.9

- Students read the questions. Stronger students can complete the questions and listen and check their answers.
- Play the CD. Students listen and complete the questions.
- Check the answers with the class. Play the CD again.

ANSWERS

See exercise 2 transcript above.

Speaking

Aim

To have a phone conversation with a friend about a summer camp

Background notes

- New York City is located on the Atlantic coast of the U.S. The city consists of five boroughs and has a population of more than eight million. It is a popular tourist destination.
- The Statue of Liberty is a famous tourist attraction in New York. The statue is situated on Liberty Island and was given to the U.S. by France as a sign of their friendship during the American Revolution.
- Rockerfeller Center is a popular tourist attraction in Manhattan, New York. People go to the top of the 70 floors for the panoramic views over the city from the top of the Rock observation deck.
- Broadway is a wide avenue in New York. It runs the length of the island of Manhattan and continues into the borough of The Bronx. One part of it is home to the theater district of the city.

Warm-up

- Ask students: *Have you ever been to a summer camp? If so, did you enjoy it? What did you do? If not, can you imagine what it might be like? Would you prefer to go to a sports camp or a theater camp?*

Exercise 4 Pairwork

- In pairs, students read the information in the adverts for the summer camps.
- If students need more help before they start their conversations, encourage them to make notes using the questions in exercise 3 and the information in the adverts.
- Students have the conversations. Remind them to look back at the questions in exercise 3 if necessary.
- Monitor and help as necessary, making sure that students are asking and answering questions correctly, using the simple present and present progressive, and that they are taking turns.
- Encourage students to make notes on their partner's answers as they will need to use this information again in exercise 5.
- Make a note of any repeated errors to go over at the end of the lesson.
- Ask one or two pairs to act out their conversations in front of the class.

ANSWERS
Students' own answers.

Writing

Aim

To make notes on what your partner is doing at the moment and then to write a postcard to a friend

Warm-up

- Ask students for a show of hands on who chose to attend the theater camp and who is attending the sports camp.

Exercise 5

- If students have made notes in exercise 4, remind them to use the notes to complete the paragraph about their partner.
- If students did not make notes in exercise 4, ask them to make them now before they complete the paragraph.
- Students can compare paragraphs in pairs.
- Ask one or two pairs to read out their completed paragraphs.

ANSWERS
Students' own answers.

Exercise 6

- Students choose one of the camps in exercise 4.
- They make notes using the information in exercise 4 to write a postcard to a friend from the camp.
- Students can write a first draft in their notebooks.
- Students swap drafts with a partner who corrects any mistakes.
- If you have blank postcards, give them out to students for them to write their final versions, or they can write them for homework in their notebooks.

Extra activity 1
- Ask students to compare postcards and to see which camp is most popular.

Extra activity 2
- You can display the final version of students' postcards around the class.

CD-ROM **WORKBOOK PAGE W7**

Grammar

be: Simple past (Affirmative, negative, questions, and short answers)

Past time expressions: *yesterday morning / afternoon / evening; last night / Monday / month / year; a year / a week / two days / twenty minutes ago*

Information questions with *was / were*

Vocabulary

Musical instruments

Musical genres

Musicians

Communication

Agreeing and disagreeing

Skills

Reading: A magazine article about a famous pop star

Listening: A radio program about a famous pop star

Speaking: Asking and answering questions about famous pop stars

Writing: A paragraph about a famous pop star

Topics

Music

Multiculturalism: Music around the world

Presentation PAGE 18

Aim

To present the new language in a motivating context

Story

Zoe is discussing a pop concert she went to. Teo couldn't go to the concert because he was playing basketball. Teo's team lost, but Sam wasn't playing. Sam appears and Teo and Zoe ask him why he couldn't play. He tells them that his parents won't let him play basketball any more because he had a bad report card.

Warm-up

- Ask students to look at the photo. Ask: *Who can you see?* (Teo, Zoe, and Sam) *Where are they?* (in town) *What do you think they are talking about?*

Exercise 1 Read and listen 1.10

- Give students time to read through the question and the answer choices before they listen.
- Play the CD. Students listen and read and choose the correct answer.
- Check the answer with the class.
- Go through the *Check it out!* box and explain the phrases.

Transcript STUDENT BOOK PAGE 18

ANSWER

b at home

Exercise 2 Comprehension

- Students read and complete the sentences with adjectives from the dialogue.
- If students need more support, ask them to underline all the adjectives in the dialogue.
- Check the answers with the class.

ANSWERS

1 electric **2** terrible **3** mad **4** bad

Consolidation

- Encourage students to make a note of any new words and phrases from the dialogue in their vocabulary books.

Language focus PAGE 19

Aim

To practice the target language in a new context

Exercise 3 Dialogue focus

- Students read the jumbled sentences and then write them in the correct order. Remind them to look back at the dialogue on page 18 if necessary.
- Do not check the answers at this point.

Exercise 4 1.11

- Play the CD. Students listen and check their answers.
- Students listen again and repeat chorally, then individually.

ANSWERS / AUDIO CD TRACK 1.11

1 Teo Were you at *The Ravens* concert last night?
  Zoe Yes, I was. It was great. The atmosphere was electric. I love rock music.
  Teo ¹Yeah, so do I. It's cool!
2 Teo There was a game yesterday.
  Zoe Oh, yeah. ²So, what was the score?
  Teo 96–32! ³We were terrible!
3 Teo ⁴Where were you last night?
  Sam I was at home.
  Teo At home? ⁵Why were you at home?
  Sam ⁶It wasn't my fault.

Exercise 5 Focus on you

- In pairs, students write their own dialogues with the expressions in the box.

ANSWERS

Students' own answers.

Exercise 6 Pairwork

- In pairs, students practice their dialogues from exercise 5.
- Monitor and check that students are asking and answering questions correctly and are swapping roles.

Vocabulary PAGE 20

Musical instruments and genres

Aim

To present and practice musical instruments and genres: *drums, guitar, harp, piano, recorder, saxophone, trumpet, violin; guitarist, harpist, trumpeter, violinist; classical, hip-hop, jazz, pop, reggae, rock*

Warm-up

- Ask students: *Do you play a musical instrument? If so, which one? If not, would you like to play one?* Elicit the names of some instruments and write them on the board.
- Ask students what kind of music they like listening to and elicit some kinds of music and write them on the board.

Exercise 1 1.12

- Give students time to look at the instruments.
- Play the CD. Students listen and write the number beside the instrument they hear.
- Play the CD a second time if necessary.
- Check the answers with the class.
- Go through the *Look!* box with the class and make sure that students understand how to form the name of the person who plays an instrument.
- Give them one or two more examples from exercise 1 and elicit the names of the players, e.g. *piano – pianist, drums – drummer, saxophone – saxophonist*.

ANSWERS
a 4 b 6 c 1 d 3 e 8 f 2 g 7 h 5

Extra activity 1
- In small groups or as a whole class activity, students choose an instrument and mime playing it. The others guess which instrument it is.

Extra activity 2
- Play *Hangman* with musical instruments. This can be done in small groups or as a whole class activity.

Extra activity 3
- Ask students to think of other musical instruments and to name them and the players, e.g. *cello – cellist, oboe – oboeist*.

Background notes

- Rihanna (picture 2), whose full name is Robyn Rihanna Fenty, was born in St Michael, Barbados in 1988. She is a pop singer, and in five years she has sold over 14 million records. *Umbrella* and *Russian Roulette* are two of her biggest hits.
- Pink Floyd (picture 3) were an English rock band who were famous in the 1960s and 1970s. They formed in 1965 and there were four members. Two of their most famous albums are *Dark side of the moon* and *Wish you were here*.

- Bob Marley (picture 5), whose real name was Robert Nesta "Bob" Marley, was a Jamaican singer-songwriter famous for his reggae music. He was born in 1945 and died in 1981. Some of his best-known hits include *No woman, no cry*, *Three little birds*, and *One love*.
- 50 Cent (picture 6), whose real name is Curtis James Jackson III, is an American rap artist from the Queens borough of New York. He was discovered by the rapper, Eminem, and he rose to fame in 2003. He has made several successful albums and more recently he has also starred in movies.

Exercise 2 1.13

- Students look at the types of music in the box and the pictures.
- Play the CD. Students listen and match the types of music with the music they hear.
- Students can compare answers in pairs.
- Check the answers with the class.

ANSWERS
2 pop 3 rock 4 classical 5 reggae 6 hip-hop

Extra activity
- Ask students to give you more examples of groups or singers who play the different genres of music.

Exercise 3 Pairwork

- In pairs, students ask and answer questions about the kind of music they like.
- Encourage them to look at the model dialogue. Monitor and help and make sure that students are taking turns to ask and answer questions.
- Encourage them to use adjectives like the ones from the dialogue on page 18, e.g. *terrible, electric*, etc.

ANSWERS
Students' own answers.

Extra activity
- Ask one or two pairs to act out their dialogues in front of the class. Encourage them to be as expressive as they can.

Consolidation
- Remind students to make a note of the new vocabulary from this lesson in their vocabulary books. Encourage them to add illustrations or translations.

CD-ROM WORKBOOK PAGE W10

Grammar PAGE 21

be: Simple past (Affirmative and negative)

Aim

To present and practice *be*: simple past, affirmative and negative forms

Warm-up

- Ask students: *Where was Zoe last night?* and elicit the affirmative answer: *She was at a concert.* Then ask students: *Where were you last night?* and elicit one or two answers.

Grammar chart / Think! box

- Go through the grammar chart with the class.
- Draw students' attention to the singular and plural forms and the fact that *was / were* are not contracted, but the negative forms *was not / were not* are (*wasn't / weren't*).
- Remind them that *was* and *were* are used to talk about situations in the past.
- Ask students to look back at the dialogue on page 18 and to find examples of the simple past.
- Students read the *Think!* box and complete the rules with the correct subject pronouns.
- Check the answers with the class.
- Remind students to check the rules on page W8.

ANSWERS

1 I   2 he   3 she   4 it   5 we   6 you   7 they

Rules PAGE W8

Exercise 1

- Students complete the sentences with *was / were* or *were / weren't*. Remind them to refer back to the grammar chart if necessary.
- They can compare answers in pairs.
- Check the answers with the class.

ANSWERS

1 weren't   2 was   3 were   4 wasn't   5 was   6 wasn't
7 were   8 wasn't

> **Extra activity**
> - If students need more practice with the affirmative form, give them some more examples of singular and plural nouns for them to say *was / were*, e.g. T: *car* S: *was*, T: *cats* S: *were*.

Past time expressions

Aim

To present and practice past time expressions

Grammar chart / Think! box

- Go through the grammar chart with the class, drawing students' attention to the different ways of saying when something happened in the past.
- Explain that past time expressions can go at the start or end of a sentence without a change in meaning.

- Ask students to look back at the dialogue on page 18 and to find an example of a past time expression.
- Refer students to the rules on page W8.

Rules PAGE W8

Exercise 2

- Students write the time expressions in the correct order, from a long time ago to the most recent.
- Students can compare answers in pairs.
- Check the answers with the class.

ANSWERS

2 three months ago   3 last week   4 two days ago
5 yesterday morning   6 yesterday evening   7 last night

> **Extra activity**
> - In small groups or as a whole class, students can make statements about where they were at certain times using the past time expressions, e.g. S1: *I was at the movies last night.* S2: *I wasn't at the movies last night. I was at home.*
> - Students can give a negative statement or they can give a different affirmative statement with a different past time expression.

Exercise 3

- Students look at the pictures and complete the sentences with *was / were*, *wasn't / weren't* and a past time expression.
- Remind students to look back at the grammar charts if necessary.
- Check the answers with the class.

ANSWERS

2 was; morning   3 weren't; ago   4 wasn't; last
5 were; last   6 wasn't; ago

Finished?

- Students guess where their partner was at certain times.
- They write sentences first before checking with their partner.
- Monitor and check that students are using *be* simple past and past time expressions correctly. Make a note of any repeated errors to go over with the class at the end of the lesson.

> **Extra activity**
> - Ask one or two pairs to report back to the class about where their partner was.

> **Consolidation**
> - Remind students to make a note of the grammar rules and explanations from this lesson in their grammar books. Encourage them to write translations and examples if it will help them to remember the grammar point.

CD-ROM WORKBOOK PAGES W10–W11

Communication PAGE 22

Agreeing and disagreeing

Aim

To present and practice the language for agreeing and disagreeing

Background notes

- 30 Seconds to Mars is an American rock band from Los Angeles. They formed in 1998 and the actor Jared Leto is their singer-songwriter. They released their third album *This is War* in 2009.
- Tokio Hotel is a four-man German rock band that formed in 2001. They have won many awards, including the 2008 Premios Latinoamérica for best international artists and song. Their fifth album, *Humanoid*, was released in 2009.
- Katy Perry, whose real name is Katherine Elizabeth Hudson, is an American singer-songwriter. She was born in 1984 in Santa Barbara, California. In 2009, she released a live album, *MTV Unplugged*.
- Daniela Mercury, whose real name is Daniela Mercuri de Almeida, is a Brazilian singer-songwriter from Salvador, Bahia. She was born in 1965. She has released many albums over the years. She is a UNICEF ambassador.
- Jay-Z, whose real name is Shawn Corey Carter, is an American hip-hop artist. He was born in 1969. He has sold more than 30 million copies of his albums in the U.S. and has received ten Grammy awards for his work.
- Nelly Furtado is a Canadian pop singer-songwriter. She was born in 1979 in Victoria, Canada, to Portuguese parents. She has sold over 22 million albums worldwide.

Warm-up

- Ask students to look at the photos and to say if they like any of the groups / singers. Encourage students to contribute their views. If possible, elicit some phrases for agreeing and disagreeing and write them on the board.

Exercise 1 🔊 1.14

- Give students time to read through the information in the chart and the dialogue.
- Play the CD. Students read and listen and check or cross the correct option.
- Stronger students can read the dialogue, check the options and then listen and check only.
- Play the CD. Students listen and check their answers.
- Students listen again and repeat.

> **ANSWERS**
>
> | | Emi | Luke |
> | ------------------- | --- | ---- |
> | 30 Seconds to Mars | ✓ | ✓ |
> | Tokio Hotel | ✓ | ✗ |
> | Katy Perry | ✗ | ✗ |
> | Daniela Mercury | ✗ | ✓ |

- Go through the *You say, You answer* box with the class. Draw students' attention to the different ways of agreeing and disagreeing.
- Ask students to find examples of the expressions in the dialogue.
- Model the sentences from the box for students to repeat chorally, then individually.

Transcript STUDENT BOOK PAGE 22

Exercise 2 Pronunciation 🔊 1.15

- Play the CD. Students listen and repeat chorally, then individually.
- Draw students' attention to the stress in each sentence and tap out the rhythm on a table if it helps.
- Ask one or two pairs to model the dialogues for the class, making sure they stress the correct words.
- Stronger students can change the words in the dialogues and use singers / groups they like / don't like themselves.

Transcript STUDENT BOOK PAGE 22

Exercise 3 🔊 1.16

- Play the CD. Students listen and check or cross the correct box.
- Students can compare answers in pairs.
- Check the answers with the class. Play the CD again if necessary.

> **ANSWERS / AUDIO CD TRACK 1.16**
>
> **Scott** Who's your favorite singer? Do you like Nelly Furtado?
> **Amy** No, I don't.
> **Scott** Really? I do. I think she's fantastic. I love pop music.
> **Amy** I like hip-hop.
> **Scott** So do I. Jay-Z is my favorite hip-hop star.
> **Amy** I like him, too.
>
> **Amy** Jay-Z ✓   Nelly Furtado ✗
> **Scott** Jay-Z ✓   Nelly Furtado ✓

> **Extra activity**
>
> - In pairs, students can act out the dialogue in exercise 3.

Exercise 4 Pairwork

- In pairs, students exchange opinions about the people.
- Monitor and check that they are taking turns to agree and disagree correctly. Make a note of any repeated errors to go over with the class at the end of the lesson.
- Ask one or two pairs to report back to the class on who their partner likes.

> **ANSWERS**
> Students' own answers.

CD-ROM WORKBOOK PAGE W12

Grammar PAGE 23

be: Simple past (Interrogative and short answers)

Aim

To present and practice the simple past of *be*: questions and short answers

Warm-up

- Ask students one or two simple past questions and elicit short answers, e.g. T: *Were you at the movies last night?* SS: *Yes, I was. / No, I wasn't.*

Grammar chart / Think! box

- Go through the grammar chart with the class. Draw students' attention to the word order in questions. Explain that we cannot contract *was* in affirmative short answers (*was / were*), unlike negative short answers (*wasn't / weren't*).
- Ask students to look back at the dialogue on page 18 and find an example of a simple past question.
- Remind students to check the rules on page W9.

Rules PAGE W9

Exercise 1

- Students write the questions and answers.
- Remind them to think about which form of the verb they need.
- Students can compare answers in pairs.
- Check the answers with the class.

ANSWERS
1 Was Abel at home yesterday? No, he wasn't.
2 Was Jessica in Brazil last summer? Yes, she was.
3 Were Jack and Ryan at the soccer game on Sunday? Yes, they were.
4 Were your cousins at the party? No, they weren't.
5 Was Johnny Depp in the movie *Avatar*? No, he wasn't.

Question words + *was / were*

Aim

To present and practice question words + *was / were*

Grammar chart / Look! box

- Go through the grammar chart with the class. Draw students' attention to the question words and word order in information questions.
- Go through the *Look!* box with the class and ask students to compare this structure with their own language.
- Direct students to the rules on page W9 if necessary.

Rules PAGE W9

Exercise 2

- Students read the answers and write the questions.
- Remind them to think about which form of the verb they need.
- Check the answers with the class.

ANSWERS
1 When were you born?
2 When were you in Spain?
3 How was the concert?
4 Where was John Lennon born?
5 Why were his parents mad?
6 How old were you in June?

Background note

- Jimi Hendrix, whose real name was James Marshall, was born in 1942 and died in 1970. He was an American singer-songwriter, but he was most famous for his guitar playing.

Exercise 3

- Students read the factfile and complete the information.
- Check the answers with the class.

ANSWERS
1 was   2 was he   3 was he born   4 November 27th, 1942

Background notes

- Ella Fitzgerald was born in 1917 and died in 1996. She was a jazz singer and is often referred to as the first Lady of Song.
- Amadeus Mozart was born in 1756 and died in 1791. One of his best-known pieces of music is his Requiem.

Exercise 4 Game!

- In pairs, students ask and answer questions about the people in the factfiles.
- Monitor and make a note of any repeated errors to go over with the class at the end of the lesson.
- Alternatively, this could be done as a gap-fill activity. One student closes their book and asks questions to find out information about Ella Fitzgerald. Students then swap roles and ask about Amadeus Mozart.

ANSWERS
Students' own answers.

> ### Extra activity
> - Students write factfiles for their favorite pop / movie / sports stars and then swap with a partner. The partner asks questions about the person and guesses who it is.

Finished?

- Students write questions about famous musicians or singers from the past.
- Nominate students to ask the class their questions.

ANSWERS
Students' own answers.

> ### Consolidation
> - Encourage students to make a note of the grammar and the rules from this lesson in their grammar books. Remind them to write example sentences or translations to help them remember the grammar.

CD-ROM WORKBOOK PAGE W11

Skills

Reading

Aim

To read and understand a magazine article about a famous pop star

Background notes

- U2 are an Irish rock band. Bono is their lead singer. They formed in 1976 when the band members were at secondary school. They have released more than ten albums and have won 22 Grammy awards, the most by any band.
- Live Aid was a rock concert that was held in 1985 in different venues, at the same time, in London, Philadelphia, Moscow, and Sydney. The concert was organized by Bob Geldof and Midge Ure.
- Amnesty International is a worldwide organization that works to protect human rights.

Warm-up

- Ask students to look at the photos and ask: *Do you know who this is?* (Bono, U2) *Do you like this band? What nationality is the band?* (Irish) *What is the name of the famous concert?* (Live Aid)

Exercise 1

- Before students read the text in detail, ask them to read it quickly and find the names of the band members and the instruments they play (Paul David Hewson (Bono) – lead singer, Larry Mullen – drummer, David Evans (The Edge) – guitarist, Adam Clayton – guitarist).
- Individually or in pairs, students read the text again and decide if the sentences are true or false. Remind them to correct the false sentences.
- Check the answers with the class.
- Encourage stronger students to give you evidence from the text for the true answers.

ANSWERS

1 True.
2 False. He was born in 1960.
3 True.
4 False. The first name of the band was Feedback.
5 False. The band's first international hit song was in 1980.
6 False. Bono was at the Live Aid concert.
7 True.

Listening

Aim

To listen to and understand information about a famous pop star

Background notes

- Elvis Presley was an American singer and actor. He was born in 1935 and died in 1977. He is often referred to as "The King".
- Mississippi is a state in the southern U.S. whose name comes from the river that flows along its west side.
- Gospel music is a type of music that expresses a personal or communal belief about Christian life.
- Blues music originated in the American deep south at the end of the 19th century. Its origins are in spiritual songs, work songs, and chants.
- Country music is a mixture of popular music forms from the south of the U.S. Its origins are found in traditional folk music, Celtic music, and gospel music.

Warm-up

- Ask students to look at the photo and ask if they know who it is (Elvis Presley) and what they know about his life.

Exercise 2 🔊 1.17

- Give students a few minutes to read the answer choices before they listen.
- Play the CD. Students listen and choose the correct answers.
- Stronger students can predict the answers and then listen and check.
- Check the answers with the class. Play the CD again if necessary.

ANSWERS / AUDIO CD TRACK 1.17

Elvis Presley was a famous rock 'n' roll singer. His nickname was "The King", because he was the king of rock 'n' roll. He was the first rock 'n' roll superstar.
Elvis was born on January 8th 1935, in the state of Mississippi. When he was a teenager his passion was music and his favorite kinds of music were gospel, blues, and country. He was a great singer and he was also very good-looking. His hair was black and his eyes were blue.
Elvis's music was popular all around the world and he was number one in the U.S. with 21 of his songs! His first hit, *Heartbreak Hotel*, is now a rock 'n' roll classic. Elvis was also the star of 33 movies, but he wasn't a great actor and people remember him for his music. Tragically, his life was very short. Elvis Presley was only 42 years old when he died in 1977.

2 a 3 a 4 b 5 c 6 c

> ### Extra activity
> - Students choose a pop star of their choice and write three multiple choice questions about them, like those in exercise 2.
> - Students give their questions to a partner. Can their partner choose the correct answers?

Speaking

Aim

To ask and answer questions about famous pop stars

Background notes

- Shakira, whose full name is Shakira Isabel Mebarak Ripoll, is a Colombian singer-songwriter. She was born in 1977 in Baranquilla, Colombia. Her major international breakthrough came in 2001 with her hit single *Wherever, Whenever*.
- Justin Timberlake is an American pop singer and actor. He was born in 1981 in Memphis, Tennessee. He was the lead singer of the pop group 'N Sync. He sold 55 million albums with 'N Sync and his first two solo albums sold more than 9 million copies worldwide.
- Baranquilla is in northern Colombia, near the Caribbean Sea. It is sometimes referred to as Colombia's Golden Gate.
- Colombia is in the north-west of South America. It has borders with Venezuela, Brazil, Ecuador, Peru and Panama. Bogotá is the capital city.
- Memphis is in the U.S. state of Tennessee, south of the Mississippi river. It is the largest city in the state.

Warm-up

- Ask students to look at the photos and ask who the people are (Shakira and Justin Timberlake). Ask students if they like their music and elicit opinions.

Exercise 3

- Students work in pairs. One student asks questions about Shakira and the other student answers. Then they swap roles and ask and answer questions about Justin Timberlake.
- Monitor and check that students are taking turns to ask and answer questions and that they are using the simple past *be* questions correctly. Make a note of any repeated errors to go over at the end of the lesson.
- Ask one or two pairs to report back to the class on what they found out about the pop stars, particularly things they did not know before.

ANSWERS
Students' own answers.

Writing

Aim

To write a paragraph about a pop star

Warm-up

- Ask students one or two questions about Shakira and see if they can remember, e.g. *Where was she born?* (Baranquilla, Colombia) *When was she born?* (1977), etc.

Exercise 4

- Students complete the paragraph with information about Shakira. Remind them to refer back to the factfile in exercise 3 if necessary.
- Stronger students can complete the paragraph from memory and then use the information in exercise 3 to check.
- Students can compare answers in pairs.
- Check the answers with the class.

ANSWERS
1 was **2** February 2nd, 1977 **3** Colombia **4** 2002 **5** was
6 *Hips Don't Lie*

Exercise 5

- Students write a paragraph about Justin Timberlake. They use the model paragraph in exercise 4 and the information in exercise 3 to help them.
- Monitor and check that students are using the information correctly and make a note of any repeated errors to go over at the end of the lesson.
- Ask one or two students to read out their paragraphs to the rest of the class.
- Students write a different paragraph about their favorite pop star.
- Remind them to make notes based on the questions in exercise 3 and to do a first draft. Students can swap drafts with a partner who corrects the mistakes.
- They can then write a final version for homework. They can add photos or illustrations if they want.
- Display the factfiles in the class.

ANSWERS
Students' own answers.

CD-ROM WORKBOOK PAGE W13

Grammar

Simple present / Present progressive
Possessive pronouns
Adverbs of manner: regular and irregular
be: Simple past (Affirmative, negative, questions, and short answers)
Past time expressions
Question words + *was* / *were*

Vocabulary

Physical descriptions
Musical instruments
Musical genres

Review A PAGES 26–27

Vocabulary

Exercise 1

ANSWERS
body: heavy, tall, thin
eyes: blue, brown, green
face: beard, freckles, glasses, mustache
hair: black, blond, brown, curly, long, red, shoulder-length, spiky, wavy

Exercise 2

ANSWERS
1 freckles 2 beard 3 glasses 4 eyes 5 heavy

Exercise 3

ANSWERS
Kinds of music: rock, hip-hop, classical, jazz, pop
Instruments: drums, guitar, harp, piano, trumpet

Grammar

Exercise 4

ANSWERS
1 A does Lally get up
 B gets up; goes
2 A Is Nathan using
 B is; 's writing
3 A Is Tomas playing
 B isn't; plays; 's playing

Exercise 5

ANSWERS
1 mine 2 hers 3 ours 4 Theirs 5 his

Exercise 6

ANSWERS
1 badly 2 slowly 3 quiet 4 fast 5 happy

Exercise 7

ANSWERS
1 late 2 happily 3 quickly 4 well 5 quietly 6 slowly

Exercise 8

ANSWERS
1 This morning the students weren't in their classroom.
2 Last year, Nikki's hair wasn't short.
3 Matt and Ellen were in the living room ten minutes ago.
4 Was Fergie your favorite singer when you were ten?
5 Were your teachers friendly at elementary school?

Background notes

- Luciano Pavarotti was an Italian opera singer from Modena. He was born in 1935 and died in 2007. He was one of the most successful tenor singers in the world.
- Miriam Makeba was a South African singer and civil rights activist. She was born in 1932 and died in 2008. She sang a mixture of jazz and traditional African music.
- ABBA was a Swedish pop group who formed in 1972. The group's name comes from the first letters of each of the band members' names. They rose to fame when they won the Eurovision Song Contest in 1974 with *Waterloo*.

Exercise 9

ANSWERS
1 1 was 2 Was 3 wasn't 4 was 5 was 6 was
2 1 was 2 was 3 was 4 was 5 was 6 was
3 1 were 2 were 3 Were 4 weren't 5 were 6 was

Got it?

Exercise 10

ANSWERS
1 were 2 was 3 was 4 'm sitting 5 'm doing
6 'm listening 7 listen 8 'm studying 9 are you doing
10 were 11 go 12 shop 13 starts 14 's calling 15 wants

Exercise 11

ANSWERS
1 She was at her grandma's 80th birthday party.
2 She's sitting in the yard and she's doing her vacation homework.
3 They were at the Kenwood Plaza shopping mall.
4 They go there two or three times a year.
5 Because he wants to check her homework.

Songs

The following songs would be appropriate to use at this point:
- *Angels* by Robbie Williams (simple present / present progressive)
- *Tom's diner* by Suzanne Vega (simple present / present progressive)
- *Thank you for the music* by ABBA (present progressive)

Grammar

Simple present / Present progressive
Possessive pronouns
Adverbs of manner: regular and irregular
be: Simple past (Affirmative, negative, questions, and short answers)
Past time expressions
Questions + *was* / *were*

Vocabulary

Physical descriptions
Musical instruments
Musical genres

Topic

Music through the ages

Culture club A `PAGE 28`

Aim

To read and understand a text about music through the ages in the U.K. and the U.S.

Background notes

- Bruce Springsteen is an American rock singer-songwriter. He was born in 1949 in New Jersey.
- Elton John is a British singer-songwriter.
- The Beatles were an English rock band who formed in Liverpool in the 1960s.
- Elvis Presley, see Unit 2, page 32.
- Pink Floyd, see Unit 2, page 28.
- Led Zeppelin were an English rock band. They sold more than 200 million albums worldwide.
- David Bowie is an English musician and actor. He was a glam rock artist in the 1970s.
- The Sex Pistols and The Clash British were punk rock bands.
- The Ramones were an American rock band who are said to have been the first punk rock band
- Queen were a British rock band who formed in 1970. Their lead singer was Freddie Mercury.
- U2, see Unit 2, page 32.
- Beyoncé is an American R&B singer-songwriter and actress. She was the lead singer with Destiny's Child.
- Jay-Z, see Unit 2, page 30.

Warm-up

- Ask students to look at the photos and ask one or two questions, e.g. *Do you know who the people are?* (Bruce Springsteen, Elton John, the Beatles) *Do you know the names of the members of the Beatles?* (George Harrison, John Lennon, Ringo Starr, and Paul McCartney).

Exercise 1

- Before students answer the questions, ask them to skim the text quickly to find the following information: *a rock band* (Pink Floyd, Led Zeppelin), *a "glam" rock star* (Elton John, David Bowie), *a punk band* (the Sex Pistols, the Clash, the Ramones), *a hip-hop star* (Beyoncé, Jay-Z).
- Students read the text and answer the questions.
- Check the answers with the class.

ANSWERS

1 It was born in the U.S. in the 1950s.
2 The Beatles were British.
3 David Bowie and Elton John were the leaders.
4 It was born in 1976.
5 The stadium rock superstars of the 1980s were Bruce Springsteen, Queen, and U2.
6 There were 130,000 people at the concert.

Exercise 2

- In pairs, students find the different kinds of music.
- Check the answers with the class.

ANSWERS

rock 'n' roll   blues   country   pop   rock   glam rock
punk rock   stadium rock   hip-hop

Exercise 3 Focus on you

- In pairs or small groups, students research two singers or bands who were important in the history of music in their country. They can do this in class or for homework.
- Encourage them to use the Internet, the school library, and the school music department.
- Encourage students to make notes on each question and to prepare a first draft of their presentation.
- Students swap drafts with a partner who corrects the mistakes.
- Students then write or prepare a final version.
- Students give their presentation to the rest of the class.

ANSWERS
Students' own answers

My progress `PAGE 29`

- For items 1–6, students read the sentences and complete the lists with their examples.
- If students have less than 3 / 5 for individual statements, encourage them to review the grammar or vocabulary and to do more practice.
- For items 7–10, students circle the answer which reflects the progress they have made in Units 1 and 2.
- If they have chosen *I'm not sure* or *No*, encourage them to review these sections and to do more practice.

You failed another test!

Grammar

Simple past: Regular verbs (Affirmative)
Simple past: Spelling variations
Simple past: Irregular verbs

Vocabulary

Jobs

Communication

Apologizing and making excuses

Skills

Reading: A history book text about a famous explorer
Listening: A biography
Speaking: A presentation on a famous person
Writing: A short paragraph about a famous person

Topics

Sport
Work
History: Famous people from the past

Presentation PAGE 30

Aim

To present the new language in a motivating context

Story

Teo and Sam are discussing why Sam isn't studying hard enough at school. Sam says he doesn't have to study to be a basketball player. Coach Carson calls Sam to his office and tells him he must do well in the math test on Wednesday or he won't play basketball for the school team again.

Warm-up

- Ask students to look at the photo and ask: *Who can you see?* (Teo, Sam, and Coach Carson) *Where are they?* (in the school gym) *What are they doing?* (Teo is talking to Sam).

Exercise 1 Read and listen 1.18

- Students read through the answer choices before they listen.
- Play the CD. Students read and listen.
- Check the answer with the class.
- Go through the dialogue and the *Check it out!* box with the class.
- Play the CD. Students listen again and repeat chorally, then individually.

Transcript STUDENT BOOK PAGE 30

ANSWER

c a basketball player

Exercise 2 Comprehension

- Students complete the sentences with the initials.
- Check the answers with the class.

ANSWERS

1 MJ 2 CC 3 CC 4 S

Consolidation

- Remind students to make a note of any new vocabulary in their vocabulary books.

Language focus PAGE 31

Aim

To practice the target language in a new context

Exercise 3 Dialogue focus

- Students read the dialogues and find the mistakes.
- Do not check answers at this point.

Exercise 4 1.19

- Play the CD. Students listen and check their answers.
- Students listen again and repeat chorally, then individually.

ANSWERS / AUDIO CD TRACK 1.19

1 **Teo** I don't believe it, Sam. You failed another <u>math</u> test. Why aren't you studying?
 Sam I don't want to be a <u>doctor</u> or a lawyer. I want to be a <u>basketball</u> player.
2 **Sam** Look at Michael Jordan. He wasn't great at school, but he played for the *Chicago Bulls* and he won <u>eight</u> NBA championships.
 Teo Michael Jordan! Are you serious? Do you think you're Michael Jordan? Get real!
3 **CC** I spoke to your <u>mom</u> yesterday.
 Sam Really? That's great. Can I play again now?
 CC I'm sorry, but you can't. You did badly <u>at school again</u>.

Exercise 5 Focus on you

- Students use the information on the cards and write about the sports personalities.
- Alternatively, students can choose the sports personality they like most and only write about that person.

ANSWERS

Students' own answers.

Exercise 6 Pairwork

- In pairs, students choose one of the personalities from exercise 5 and describe them to a partner.
- Ask some pairs to tell the class about their personalities.

ANSWERS

Students' own answers.

Vocabulary PAGE 32

Jobs

Aim

To present and practice vocabulary for jobs: *accountant, doctor, electrician, engineer, factory worker, hairdresser, journalist, lawyer, office worker, postal worker, salesclerk, teacher*

Warm-up

- Ask students one or two questions about jobs, e.g. *What's my job? What job does your dad do? Your mom?*

Exercise 1 1.20

- Students match the pictures with the words in the box.
- Play the CD. Students listen and check their answers.
- Students listen again and repeat chorally, then individually.

ANSWERS / AUDIO CD TRACK 1.20

1	journalist	7	salesclerk
2	postal worker	8	engineer
3	teacher	9	hairdresser
4	doctor	10	lawyer
5	accountant	11	factory worker
6	electrician	12	office worker

Extra activity

- In small groups or as a whole class, students choose a job and mime it. The others guess which job it is.

Exercise 2

- Go through the *Look!* box with the class.
- Elicit or give an example for each ending, e.g. *teacher, pianist, electrician, businessman, actor.*
- Students complete the endings with examples from exercise 1.
- Check the answers with the class.

ANSWERS

1 journalist   2 electrician   3 accountant   4 doctor

Extra activity

- In small groups or as a whole class, students see how many more jobs they can think of for each ending. You can write the jobs on the board under each ending. For example: *artist, politician, flight attendant, inventor.*

Exercise 3

- Students write the names of the jobs.
- Remind them to look back at the jobs in exercise 1 if necessary.
- Students can compare answers in pairs.
- Check the answers with the class.

ANSWERS

2 journalist   3 hairdresser   4 postal worker   5 engineer
6 factory worker

Extra activity

- Students write definitions for the remaining jobs in exercise 1. Encourage them to use dictionaries if they need help with vocabulary.
- They swap definitions with a partner and guess the jobs.
- Alternatively, ask volunteers to read out their definition to the class and the class guesses which job it is.

Exercise 4 Pairwork

- In pairs, students talk about jobs they want to do when they leave school.
- Monitor and help as necessary, making sure that students are taking turns to ask and answer questions.
- Ask one or two pairs to report back to the class. Are there any interesting jobs?

Consolidation

- Remind students to make a note of the vocabulary from the lesson in their vocabulary books. Encourage them to illustrate the jobs or to add translations to help them remember them.

CD-ROM   **WORKBOOK PAGE W16**

Grammar PAGE 33

Simple past: Regular verbs (Affirmative)

Aim

To present and practice the simple past affirmative of regular verbs

Warm-up

- Write the word *play* on the board and elicit or give the simple past *played*.

Grammar chart

- Go through the grammar chart with the class. Ask students what they notice about the ending for the simple past regular verb *play*. Draw students' attention to the fact that it is the same form for all persons.
- Ask students to look back at the dialogue on page 30 and find an example of a simple past regular verb.
- Refer them to the rules on page W14 if necessary.
- Students read the *Think!* box and choose the correct ending.
- Check the answer with the class.

ANSWER
that started and finished in the past

Rules PAGE W14

Exercise 1

- Students complete the sentences with the simple past form of the verbs in the box.
- Check the answers with the class.

ANSWERS
1 listened 2 helped 3 started 4 asked 5 washed
6 waited 7 opened 8 talked

> **Extra activity**
> - If students need more practice with the simple past regular form, call out the verbs from the box in exercise 1 again for students to give you the simple past form.
> - Alternatively, you can do this with different verbs to reinforce the -ed ending.

Simple past: Spelling variations

Aim

To present and practice simple present spelling variations

Grammar chart

- Go through the grammar chart with the class.
- Elicit or give one more verb for each rule, e.g. + **-ed** *asked*, **-y** + **-ied** *tried*, **double consonant** + **-ed** *planned*.
- Refer students to the rules on page W14 if necessary.

Rules PAGE W14

Exercise 2

- Students read and complete the sentences with the simple past form of the verbs in the box.
- Monitor and check that students are using the spelling rules correctly.

- Check the answers with the class.

ANSWERS
1 1 stopped 2 arrived
2 1 studied 2 helped 3 called 4 talked

Exercise 3 Pronunciation 🎵 1.21

- Play the CD. Students listen and repeat chorally, then individually.
- Ask students about the pronunciation of each ending and elicit or give the rules.
- Remind them to check the rules on page W14.

Transcript STUDENT BOOK PAGE 33

Rules PAGE W14

Exercise 4 🎵 1.22

- Play the CD. Students listen and write the verbs in the correct column.
- Stronger students can put the verbs in the correct column and then listen and check.
- Check the answers with the class.
- Students listen again and repeat chorally, then individually.

ANSWERS / AUDIO CD TRACK 1.22
lived /d/   helped /t/   decided /ɪd/
talked /t/   started /ɪd/   watched /t/
needed /ɪd/   ended /ɪd/   opened /d/

1 opened 2 talked 3 watched
4 started 5 needed 6 ended

> **Extra activity**
> - In pairs or as a whole class, call out the base form of a verb from the lesson. Ask students to give you the simple past and the pronunciation of the ending, e.g. T: *cry* S1: *cried* S2: /d/.

Finished?

- Students write sentences about what they did yesterday evening and last Saturday using the verbs from the lesson.
- In pairs, students tell each other what they did.
- Ask one or two pairs to report back to the class.

ANSWERS
Students' own answers.

> **Extra activity**
> - In small groups or as a whole class, students tell a story using the simple past, e.g. *Last night I went to bed at 11 p.m. I heard a noise …*
> - Students can continue from this point or they can begin in their own way.

> **Consolidation**
> - Remind students to make a note of the grammar and the rules from this lesson in their grammar books. Encourage them to write examples or translations that will help them remember.

CD-ROM WORKBOOK PAGE W16

Communication PAGE 34

Apologizing and making excuses

Aim

To present and practice the language for apologizing and making excuses

Warm-up

* Ask students if they know what to say in English if they make a mistake, and elicit or give: *I'm sorry.*

Exercise 1 📀 1.23

* Before students listen, give them a few minutes to read the answer choices.
* Play the CD. Students listen and choose the correct answers.
* Check the answers with the class.
* Play the CD. Students listen again and repeat chorally, then individually.

ANSWERS / AUDIO CD TRACK 1.23

1 **David**	Excuse me, Mr. Clarke.
Mr. Clarke	Yes, David. What is it?
David	I'm sorry, but I don't have my [1]English book.
Mr. Clarke	Where is it?
David	I left it [2]at home.
Mr. Clarke	Never mind. [3]Work with Naomi.
David	Thanks, Mr. Clarke.
2 **Pam**	Hi, Sal. Do you have my Red Hot Chili Peppers [1]CD?
Sal	Oh, I'm sorry. It's at [2]home.
Pam	It doesn't matter. Give it to me on [3]Monday.

* Go through the *You say, You answer* box with the class. Ask students to find examples of the expressions in the dialogue. Draw students' attention to the different ways of responding to an apology.
* Ask one or two pairs to act out the conversations for the rest of the class.

Exercise 2 Pronunciation 📀 1.24

* Play the CD. Students listen and repeat chorally, then individually.
* If students need more practice, write the words and sounds on the board and pronounce them in an exaggerated way. Draw students' attention to the shape the lips make to produce these sounds.

Transcript STUDENT BOOK PAGE 34

Exercise 3 📀 1.25

* Play the CD. Students listen and write the words in the correct row according to the pronunciation.
* Stronger students can read the words and write them in the correct row, then listen and check.
* Students can compare answers in pairs.
* Check the answers with the class. You can write the sounds on the board and ask volunteers to come out and write the words under the correct sound.

ANSWERS / AUDIO CD TRACK 1.25

hot /ɒ/   home /oʊ/   sorry /ɒ/   photo /oʊ/   stop /ɒ/
go /oʊ/   don't /oʊ/   got /ɒ/   on /ɒ/   woke /oʊ/

1 sorry   2 stop   3 got   4 on
5 photo   6 go   7 don't   8 woke

> ### Extra activity
> * If students need more practice, call out words from exercise 3 in a different order for them to say the correct sound.

Exercise 4 📀 1.26

* Give students a few minutes to read the answer choices.
* Play the CD. Students listen and choose the correct answers.
* Students can compare answers in pairs.
* Check the answers with the class.

ANSWERS / AUDIO CD TRACK 1.26

1 **Megan**	Beth, can you play tennis with me this afternoon?
Beth	I'm really sorry, Megan, but I can't. I have a piano lesson at three o'clock.
Megan	Don't worry. Let's play tomorrow.
Beth	OK.
2 **Alex**	Mom!
Mom	Yes, Alex. What is it?
Alex	Don't get mad, but I left my jacket on the bus.
Mom	You what?
Alex	I left my jacket on the bus. I'm sorry.
Mom	Oh, Alex. That jacket's new and it was expensive. Call the bus station now!
3 **Toby**	Excuse me, Mrs. Parkinson.
Mrs. Parkinson	Yes, Toby. What's the problem?
Toby	I'm sorry, Mrs. Parkinson, but I forgot my geography book. I thought we had history today.
Mrs. Parkinson	Never mind, Toby. You can sit with Henry and look at his book.
4 **Miss Taylor**	You're late, Emma. The lesson started five minutes ago.
Emma	I'm sorry, Miss Taylor. I woke up late. Can I come in?
Miss Taylor	Yes, you can.
Emma	Thank you, Miss Taylor. I'm really sorry.

2 c   3 c   4 a

Exercise 5 Pairwork

* In pairs, students take turns to apologize for one of the actions in the box and then to reply. Remind them to refer back to the *You say, You answer* box in exercise 1.

CD-ROM WORKBOOK PAGE W18

Grammar PAGE 35

Simple past: Irregular verbs

Aim

To present and practice the simple past of irregular verbs

Warm-up

- Write one or two base forms on the board and elicit the irregular simple past, e.g. *come – came*.

Grammar chart

- Go through the grammar chart as a class. Draw students' attention to the different forms and explain that there are no patterns for irregular forms.
- Ask students to look back at the dialogue on page 30 to find an example of a simple past irregular verb.
- Give students a few minutes to try and work out how the words change. Refer them to the rules on page W15 to check.
- Remind them that the simple past is the same form for all persons.

Rules PAGE W15

Exercise 1

- Students complete the sentences with the simple past form of the verbs.
- Remind students to check the grammar chart if necessary.
- Check the answers with the class.

ANSWERS
1 wrote 2 read 3 took 4 saw 5 made 6 went

Extra activity
• If students need more practice with the irregular forms, call out the base forms from the grammar chart for students to give you the simple past form.

Exercise 2

- Students read and complete the message with the simple past form of the verbs.
- Remind them that the simple past of *be* is *was / were*.
- Students can compare answers in pairs.
- Check the answers with the class.

ANSWERS
1 had 2 tried 3 went 4 took 5 saw 6 met
7 spoke 8 was 9 ate

Extra activity
• Read out the message, stopping at each gap for students to give you the correct verb.
• Alternatively, you could use the completed text as a dictation and read it out sentence by sentence.

Background notes

- Rubens Barrichello is a Brazilian Formula 1 driver. He was born in 1972 in São Paulo. He is said to be one of the most experienced drivers in F1 history and was a protégé of the late Ayrton Senna.
- São Paulo is the largest city in Brazil and it is the capital of the state of São Paulo, the most populous Brazilian state.
- Formula 3 is a type of open-wheel formula racing. Formula 3 racing forms an important step in the careers of Formula 1 drivers.
- The Formula 1 season consists of a series of races around the world called Grand Prix races. They take place on specially built circuits, with the cars travelling up to 360 km per hour.
- Jordan, Stewart, Ferrari, Honda, and Williams-Cosworth are all sponsors of Formula 1 racing cars.

Exercise 3

- Students complete the text with the simple past forms of the verbs.
- Remind them that not all the verbs are irregular.
- Check the answers with the class.

ANSWERS
1 loved 2 had 3 rode 4 gave 5 started 6 came
7 became 8 left 9 traveled 10 won

Extra activity
• Students can research another sports personality or pop star and write a short text about their life, using the text in exercise 3 as a model.

Exercise 4 Game!

- In groups of three, students make a story using the simple past of the verbs in the list. They must repeat the sentence the student before them says and add a new one each time.
- Monitor and check that students are using the simple past correctly and make a note of any errors to go over at the end of the lesson.
- Ask groups to tell their stories to the rest of the class.

ANSWERS
Students' own answers.

Extra activity
• Ask students to vote for the best story.

Finished?

- Students write their stories from exercise 4. They can add illustrations if they wish.

ANSWERS
Students' own answers.

CD-ROM WORKBOOK PAGES W16–W17

Skills PAGES 36–37

Reading

Aim

To read and understand a history book text about a famous explorer

Warm-up

- Ask students if they know anything about Christopher Columbus. If so, elicit the information and write it on the board.

Background notes

- Christopher Columbus was an Italian explorer from the 15th century. His voyages across the Atlantic led to the discovery of the Americas.
- Genoa is an important seaport in the north of Italy. It is thought that Christopher Columbus was born there.
- Cuba is an island country in the Caribbean. Spanish is the official language on the island, although the island declared itself independent from Spain in 1868.
- San Salvador is the capital city and the largest city in El Salvador, in Central America.
- Spain is in south-west Europe on the Iberian Peninsula. The Canary Islands, the Balearic Islands, and the cities of Ceuta and Melilla in North Africa also belong to Spain.
- Africa is the world's second largest continent (Asia is the largest). It covers about six percent of the Earth's total surface. There are 53 countries in Africa.

Exercise 1

- Before students read the text in detail, ask them to skim the text and to find out the following: the names of three ships (the *Niña*, the *Pinta*, the *Santa Maria*) and two dates (August 3rd 1942, the day the ships left Spain, and October 12th, Columbus Day).
- Students read the text and complete the summary.
- Remind them to read the summary before they complete it. Encourage them to think about the meaning of the whole sentence before they fill in each gap.
- Students can compare answers in pairs.
- Check the answers with the class.

ANSWERS

1 round   2 west   3 King Ferdinand   4 three   5 months
6 India   7 Caribbean   8 Spain   9 plants   10 October

Extra activity

- Give students a few minutes to read and memorize the details from the text.
- In small groups, ask students the following questions: *Where was Columbus born?* (Genoa) *Who were the king and queen of Spain in 1492?* (Ferdinand and Isabella) *What did they give Columbus?* (money for the journey) *What was the name of the island he landed on?* (San Salvador) *Where was the island?* (in the Caribbean) *Name two things he took back to Spain.* (gold, plants, or animals).
- The group with the most correct answers is the winner.

Listening

Aim

To listen to and understand information about the life of George Washington

Background notes

- George Washington was the first president of the U.S. He was born in 1732 and died in 1799.

Warm-up

- Ask students to look at the picture and ask who it is (George Washington). Elicit any more details about him.

Exercise 2 🔘 1.27

- Give students a few minutes to read the answer choices before they listen
- Play the CD. Students listen and choose the correct answers.
- Check the answers with the class.

ANSWERS / AUDIO CD TRACK 1.27

George Washington was born on February 22nd, <u>1732</u>, on a farm in Virginia. At the time, America wasn't an independent country. It was a <u>British colony.</u>
When Washington was <u>20</u> years old he joined the army and fought in a war to protect British land from <u>French people and some Indian tribes</u>. The British won the war and Washington became a colonel in the army.
In the 1770s, <u>American colonists</u> wanted to be free from Britain and <u>asked George Washington to be the Commander</u> of their army. They declared their independence in <u>1776</u> and started a war against Britain called the War of Independence. In 1781, the Americans won the war and formed the United States of America. Washington became <u>the first American President</u> in 1789. He was President for <u>eight</u> years, but in 1797 he left politics and returned to his farm in Virginia. He died there in 1799.

1 British   2 20   3 French and Indian people   4 1776
5 American army   6 first   7 eight

Extra activity

- Read the first paragraph of the transcript out sentence by sentence for students to write down.
- Check the answers with the class.

Consolidation

- Encourage students to make a note of any new vocabulary from the reading and listening texts in their vocabulary books.

Speaking

Aim

To give an oral presentation on a famous person

Background notes

- William Shakespeare was an English poet and playwright. He was born in Stratford-upon-Avon, but the exact date of his birth is unknown. He died in 1616. He is said to be one of the greatest writers in the English language and he wrote comedies and tragedies. His plays include *Romeo and Juliet, the Merchant of Venice*, and *Hamlet*.
- Marie Curie was a Polish physicist and chemist. She was awarded Nobel prizes in physics and chemistry. She was born in Warsaw in 1867 and died in 1934. She is said to have created the theory of radioactivity and she helped establish some of the first studies into the treatment of certain types of cancer. Her husband was Pierre Curie, a French physicist.

Warm-up

- Ask students to look at the pictures and ask: *Do you know the people? Who are they?* (William Shakespeare and Marie Curie) *Where were they from?* (Shakespeare was from the U.K. and Marie Curie was from Poland).

Exercise 3

- In pairs or small groups, students choose one of the people and make notes about their lives.
- They prepare an oral presentation from their notes. Encourage them to expand their notes into full sentences and refer them back to the listening text in exercise 2 if necessary.
- Students can practice in pairs or groups.
- Ask one or two pairs or groups to give their presentation to the class.

ANSWERS

Students' own answers.

> **Extra activity**
> - Students can ask questions about the person in the oral presentation. The speaker answers the questions.

Writing

Aim

To write a short paragraph about a famous person's life

Warm-up

- Ask students: *What do you remember about Shakespeare and Marie Curie?*

Exercise 4

- Individually or in pairs, students plan their paragraph using their notes from exercise 3.
- Remind them to think about the structure and the order of the information in their paragraphs. They can refer back to the reading text in exercise 1 if necessary.
- Students write a first draft and swap with a partner or another pair.
- The partner corrects any mistakes.
- Students write a final draft of their paragraphs in class or for homework.
- Encourage them to add a picture or photo to their final version.

> **Extra activity**
> - Students can research a famous person of their choice and write a paragraph about them.
> - The paragraphs can be displayed in the classroom.

CD-ROM WORKBOOK PAGE W19

4 What did you do last night?

Grammar

Simple past: Negative

Simple past: Interrogative and short answers

Question words + Simple past: *what, where, who, why*

Vocabulary

Movies

Communication

Buying a movie ticket

Skills

Reading: A magazine article about a movie star

Listening: Two teenagers discussing a movie

Speaking: To ask and answer questions about movies

Writing: A short text about two movies

Topics

Multiculturalism: Movies people like to watch

Presentation PAGE 38

Aim

To present the new language in a motivating context

Story

Sam and Zoe are discussing what they did the night before. Zoe watched *Spider-Man 3* on TV. Sam says he didn't watch it because he saw it at the movies ages ago and didn't like it. They then discuss what movies they like and Zoe invites Sam to watch a DVD at her house. At first he refuses, saying he has a math test, but then changes his mind.

Warm-up

- Ask students to look at the photo and ask: *Who can you see?* (Sam and Zoe) *Where are they?* (at school) *What do you think they are talking about?*

Exercise 1 Read and listen 1.28

- Students read through the answer choices before they listen.
- Play the CD. Students read and listen and choose the correct answer.
- Check the answer with the class.
- Go through the dialogue and the *Check it out!* box.
- Students listen again and repeat chorally, then individually.

Transcript STUDENT BOOK PAGE 38

ANSWER

c movies

Exercise 2 Comprehension

- Students read the dialogue again and answer the questions.
- Play the CD again. Students can compare answers in pairs.
- Check the answers with the class.

ANSWERS

1 Her favorite actor is Tobey Maguire.
2 His favorite movies are *Sherlock Holmes* and *Star Trek* / action and science fiction movies.
3 They decide to watch *Alice In Wonderland* on DVD.

Extra activity

- In pairs, students can act out the dialogue. Ask one or two pairs to act it out for the rest of the class.

Consolidation

- Remind students to make a note of any new words or phrases in their vocabulary books.

Language focus PAGE 39

Aim

To practice the target language in a new context

Exercise 3 Dialogue focus

- In pairs, students read the dialogues and put them in the correct order.
- Remind them to look back at the dialogue in exercise 1 if necessary. Do not check the answers at this point.

Exercise 4 🔘 1.29

- Play the CD. Students listen and check their answers.
- Students listen again and repeat chorally, then individually.

ANSWERS / AUDIO CD TRACK 1.29

1 **Sam** What did you do last night?
  Zoe I watched *Spider-Man 3* on TV. Did you watch it?
  Sam No, I didn't. I didn't watch TV last night.
2 **Sam** I saw it at the movies ages ago! I didn't like it. It was awful. Did you like it?
  Zoe Yes, I did. I love Tobey Maguire! He's my favorite actor!
  Sam Did you like the movie, or did you like Tobey Maguire?
  Zoe I liked them both!
3 **Zoe** What kind of movies do you like?
  Sam I like action and science fiction movies. My favorite movies are *Sherlock Holmes* and *Star Trek*. I bet you like love stories!
  Zoe Yes, but I like fantasy movies, too.

Exercise 5 Focus on you

- Students read the example dialogue and then write similar dialogues using the activities in the box.
- Remind them to use the simple past.

ANSWERS

Students' own answers.

Exercise 6 Pairwork

- In pairs, students practice their dialogues from exercise 5.
- Monitor and check that they are using the simple past.

ANSWERS

Students' own answers.

Vocabulary PAGE 40

Movies

Aim

To present and practice movie vocabulary: *action movie, animated movie, comedy, fantasy movie, horror movie, love story, science fiction movie, thriller*

Warm-up

- Ask students to look at the movie stills and ask: *Do you know the names of the movies? Have you seen any of them?* and elicit replies.

Exercise 1

- Students match the pictures with the movies in the box.
- Students can compare answers in pairs. Do not check the answers at this point.
- Draw students' attention to the *Look!* box so they can see when the word *movie* is used with which movie types.

Exercise 2 💿 1.30

- Play the CD. Students listen and check their answers to exercise 1.
- Students listen again and repeat chorally, then individually.

ANSWERS / AUDIO CD TRACK 1.30

1 science fiction movie   2 animated movie   3 action movie
4 love story   5 horror movie   6 fantasy movie   7 comedy
8 thriller

Exercise 3 💿 1.31

- Play the CD. Students listen to the movie extracts and guess what kind of movie they come from.
- Students can compare answers in pairs. Play the CD again if necessary.
- Check the answers with the class.

ANSWERS / AUDIO CD TRACK 1.31

1 **Man**	I missed you so much when I was away!
Woman	Me too, my darling. It was an eternity!
Man	I never want to leave you again. Giulia, my love. Giulia, will you marry me?
Woman	Oh, Alfredo! Yes, yes!
2 **Man**	R3T3. Where is planet Zikton?
Robot	My radar system indicates that it isn't in our solar system.
Man	Is it near our galaxy?
Robot	Yes, it is. It's about twenty light years from here.
Man	And what are life conditions like there?
Robot	The life conditions are similar to those on planet Earth.
Man	Good. Set our course for planet Zikton!
3 **Woman**	Oh no! They're behind us!
Man	OK, hang on!
Woman	OK, I can't see them now. Oh no! There they are!
Man	Get down! They have a gun!
Second man	It's the police! Let's get out of here!

4 **Woman**	Hello? Hello, who's there? Who is it? Hello? Hello? Kevin? Where are you? There's something wrong with the phone. Kevin? Kevin, where are you? Oh, no! The lights! I can't see anything! Kevin! Kevin!
5 **Scott**	Gosh, Katie, you're my best friend! It's great to talk! I can call you with all my problems and you always listen to me! Katie? Katie? I don't believe it! She put the phone down!
Mark	So what's new, Scott? Katie never listens to you anyway. Why don't you talk to the telephone?!
Woman	Mark, that is just typical! Talk to the telephone! That's crazy! I don't believe it … men!
Mark	I'm going out!
Woman	So, Scott … can I call you TELE – phone or do you prefer phone?
6 **Narrator**	Our story begins a long, long time ago in the far, far away kingdom of Fantastica. Here a young he-boy, Atruya, lives with his old grandma, helping her to look after their small house. Atruya doesn't know it, but he has super powers. One night, Atruya wakes from a very deep sleep, only to find …

2 science fiction movie   3 action movie   4 thriller
5 comedy   6 fantasy movie

Background notes

- *Ponyo* is a 2008 Japanese animated movie. Ponyo is a goldfish who becomes the friend of a human boy. It was released in the U.S. in 2009.
- *X-Men Origins: Wolverine* is a movie released in 2009. It is based on an American superhero from Marvel comics. The movie is a prequel to the X-Men movie series.

Exercise 4 Pairwork

- In pairs, students tell their partner about their favorite kinds of movie.
- Monitor and check that students are using movie vocabulary correctly.
- Ask one or two pairs to report back to the class.

ANSWERS
Students' own answers.

Extra activity
- Students design a poster for their favorite movie or for an invented movie.

Consolidation
- Remind students to make a note of the vocabulary from the lesson in their vocabulary books. Tell them that it can be useful to give an example for each kind of movie.

CD-ROM   **WORKBOOK PAGE W22**

Grammar PAGE 41

Simple past (Negative)

Aim

To present and practice the simple past negative

Warm-up

- Make simple past affirmative statements and elicit or give the negative form, e.g. *I watched TV last night. I didn't watch TV last night.*

Grammar chart / Think! box

- Go through the grammar chart with the class.
- Draw students' attention to the use of the full and short forms of *did not* for the simple past negative form. Remind them that the form is the same for all persons, and that the simple past negative is formed the same way for regular and irregular verbs.
- Ask students to look back at the dialogue on page 38 and find an example of the simple past negative form.
- Students read and complete the *Think!* box.
- Check the answers with the class.
- Refer students to the rules on page W20 if necessary.

ANSWERS
1 didn't play
2 didn't drink
3 didn't win
4 in the same way

Rules PAGE W20

Exercise 1

- Students rewrite the affirmative sentences in the negative.
- Remind them to check the grammar chart if necessary.
- Students can compare answers in pairs.
- Check the answers with the class.

ANSWERS
1 You didn't sing that song very well.
2 Jake didn't go to school yesterday.
3 Mari didn't wear her new jeans to the party.
4 Ana and Luis didn't play tennis on Monday.
5 I didn't like *Avatar* very much.
6 We didn't buy popcorn at the movie theater.

Extra activity
- If students need more practice, call out an affirmative simple past form for students to give you the negative form.

Exercise 2

- Students rewrite the sentences using the true information in parentheses.
- Students can compare answers in pairs.
- Check the answers with the class.

ANSWERS
1 Alfred Hitchcock didn't direct love stories. He directed thrillers.
2 Ben Stiller didn't star in *Star Wars*. He starred in *Night at the Museum*.
3 Corbin Bleu didn't play the part of Troy in *High School Musical*. Zac Efron played the part of Troy.
4 Madonna didn't sing in the musical *Hairspray*. John Travolta sang in *Hairspray*.
5 Disney didn't make the cartoon *Monsters vs. Aliens*. Dreamworks made the cartoon *Monsters vs. Aliens*.
6 Mike Myers wasn't the voice of Donkey in *Shrek*. Eddie Murphy was the voice of Donkey.

Exercise 3

- Students complete the message with the simple past affirmative or negative form of the verbs.
- Remind them to think carefully about regular and irregular verbs and to check the rules on page 122 if necessary.
- Check the answers with the class.

ANSWERS
1 arrived   2 tried   3 didn't have   4 didn't go   5 got up
6 went   7 wanted   8 didn't take   9 didn't buy

Finished?

- Students check and cross the things they did/didn't do yesterday and then write sentences.
- They can compare sentences in pairs.
- Ask one or two pairs to read out their sentences to the rest of the class.

ANSWERS
Students' own answers.

Consolidation
- Remind students to make a note of the grammar rules and examples from this lesson in their grammar books.

CD-ROM WORKBOOK PAGE W20

Communication PAGE 42

Buying a movie ticket

Aim

To present and practice the language for buying a movie ticket

Warm-up

- Ask students questions about the movies and elicit replies, e.g. *How often do you go to the movies? Who do you go with? How much are the tickets?*

Exercise 1 ⓒ 1.32

- Give students time to look at the numbers before they listen.
- Play the CD. Students listen and read and write the numbers in the correct place in the dialogue.
- Students can compare answers in pairs.
- Check the answers with the class.
- Students listen again and repeat chorally, then individually.

ANSWERS / AUDIO CD TRACK 1.32

Man	What time is the next showing of *Up*, please?
Woman	It's at 8 p.m.
Man	OK. Can I have ¹1 adult ticket and ²2 children's tickets, please?
Woman	Yes, sure. Where do you want to sit?
Man	In the center, please.
Woman	OK. That's ³25 dollars.
Man	Here you are.
Woman	⁴30 dollars. Thank you. Here are your tickets and ⁵5 dollars change.
Man	Which screen is it, please?
Woman	It's screen ⁶seven.
Man	Thanks.

1 1 2 2 3 16 4 20 5 4 6 7

- Go through the *You ask, You answer* box with the class. Draw students' attention to the different ways of asking and answering questions.
- Ask students to look back at the dialogue and to find the phrases.
- In pairs, students practice asking and answering questions using the information in the box.
- Stronger students can change the information and use their own ideas.

Exercise 2 Pronunciation ⓒ 1.33

- Go through the pronunciation box with the class.
- Play the CD. Students listen and repeat chorally and individually.
- Play the CD again if necessary.

Transcript STUDENT BOOK PAGE 42

Exercise 3 ⓒ 1.34

- Play the CD. Students listen and choose the correct answers.
- Students listen again and repeat chorally, then individually.

ANSWERS / AUDIO CD TRACK 1.34

1 Here's your change.
2 I'd like to sit in the center, please.
3 I'd like to buy one ticket, please.
1 c /t ʃ/   2 a /s/   3 b /k/

Extra activity

- If students need more practice with these sounds, call out words in exercise 2 again in a different order and ask them to identify the sound.

Background notes

- *Harry Potter and the Deathly Hallows Part 1* (released in 2010) and *Harry Potter and the Deathly Hallows Part 2* (released in 2011) are the final movies in the Harry Potter series.
- *Fantastic Mr. Fox* is a 2009 movie, directed by Wes Anderson, based on the Roald Dahl novel. George Clooney and Meryl Streep were the voices of Mr. and Mrs. Fox.

Exercise 4 Pairwork

- In pairs, students write and practice dialogues, using the prompts.
- Monitor and check that they are using the correct questions and answers. Remind them to look back at the dialogue in exercise 1 if necessary.
- Ask one or two pairs to act out their dialogue in front of the class.

ANSWERS
Students' own answers.

Consolidation

- Remind students to make a note of any new words and phrases from this lesson in their vocabulary books.

CD-ROM WORKBOOK PAGE W24

Grammar `PAGE 43`

Simple past (Interrogative and short answers)

Aim

To present and practice simple past interrogative and short answers

Warm-up

- Ask students simple past questions and elicit short answers, e.g. T: *Dani, did you go to the movies last night?* SS: *Yes, I did. / No, I didn't.*

Grammar chart

- Go through the grammar chart with the class. Draw students' attention to the use of *did* in the interrogative and the word order. Highlight the fact that the main verb is not repeated in short answers. Remind them that the form is the same for regular and irregular verbs.
- Ask students to look back at the dialogue on page 38 to find an example of a simple past interrogative and short answer.
- Refer them to the rules on page W20 if necessary.

Rules `PAGE W20`

Exercise 1

- Students write simple past questions and short answers.
- Remind them to use *did* and to think about the base form of the verb.
- Students can compare answers in pairs.
- Check the answers with the class.

ANSWERS

1 Did Louise make a pizza at the weekend? No, she didn't.
2 Did Danny buy a sweatshirt on Saturday morning? Yes, he did.
3 Did Neil and Sarah watch a horror movie last night? No, they didn't.
4 Did Sofia go to school yesterday? No, she didn't.
5 Did the team win the game? Yes, it / they did.

> **Extra activity**
>
> - In small groups, one student thinks of something they did yesterday. The others ask a maximum of ten simple past questions to guess the activity. The student answering can only give short answers, e.g. S2: *Did you go to the movies yesterday?* S1: *No, I didn't.*
> - The student who guesses the activity takes the next turn.

Question words + Simple past

Aim

To present and practice question words + simple past

Warm-up

- Ask one or two simple past questions and elicit simple past answers, e.g. T: *What did you do last night, Alicia?* SS: *I went to Sandra's house.*

Grammar chart

- Go through the grammar chart with the class. Draw students' attention to the question words and the word order.
- Ask students to look back at the dialogue on page 38 and find an example of this type of question.
- Refer them to the rules on page W21 if necessary.

Rules `PAGE W21`

Exercise 2

- Students complete the interview, using the simple past form of the verbs in parentheses.
- Remind them to think carefully about the simple past form they need to use. Explain that they will need to use affirmative, negative, and interrogative forms and short forms.
- Students can compare answers in pairs.
- Check the answers with the class.

ANSWERS

1 didn't buy 2 won 3 was 4 Who did you give
5 gave 6 loved 7 was 8 What did you do 9 had
10 didn't stay 11 saw 12 Did you like 13 did 14 loved
15 Did you meet 16 didn't 17 wanted 18 waited
19 didn't see 20 left

Exercise 3 Game!

- In small teams, students write simple past questions with the words.
- Students then have three minutes to ask people in different teams their questions and get the answers.
- Monitor and check that students are asking and answering questions correctly. Make a note of any repeated errors to go over with the class at the end of the lesson.
- The team with the most points is the winner.

ANSWERS
Students' own answers.

Finished?

- Students write five simple past questions to ask their partner.
- They ask their partner their questions and make a note of the replies.
- Pairs can report back to the class.

ANSWERS
Students' own answers.

> **Consolidation**
>
> - Remind students to make a note of the grammar rules and examples from this lesson in their grammar books. Encourage them to write translations or their own examples if it will help them remember the grammar more easily.

CD-ROM `WORKBOOK PAGE W23`

Skills PAGES 44–45

Reading

Aim

To read and understand a magazine article about a movie star

Background notes

- Harrison Ford is an American actor and movie producer.
- *The X-Files* is a Canadian-American science fiction TV series that was first shown in 1993.
- The Walt Disney Company is the largest media and entertainment company in the world. It was founded in 1923 by Walt and Roy Disney.
- *Even Stevens* was an American TV comedy show.
- An Emmy award is a famous TV production award.
- *Holes* was a 2003 Disney movie directed by Andrew Davis. It stars Shia LaBeouf, Sigourney Weaver, and Jon Voight.
- Steven Spielberg is an American movie producer and director. He is well known for his science fiction and action movies, which include *Jaws*, *E.T*, and *Jurassic Park*.

Warm-up

- Ask students to look at the photos and ask: *Do you know who the actor is?* (Shia LaBoeuf) *Which movies did he star in?* ("Transformers", "Indian Jones") *Do you like him / his movies?*

Exercise 1

- Students read the text and complete the interview with the missing questions.
- Encourage them to look carefully at the answers to help them work out which question is appropriate.
- Check the answers with the class.

ANSWERS

1 When did Shia start to act?
2 When did he become famous?
3 When did he have his first movie role?
4 What's the secret of Shia's success?

Exercise 2

- Students read the text again and answer the questions.
- Remind them to look at key words in the questions and to think about the type of information they will need in the answers, e.g. numbers, dates, names, etc.
- Check the answers with the class.

ANSWERS

1 He appeared in *The X-Files* when he was twelve.
2 He played the part of Louis Stevens.
3 He won an Emmy award.
4 Because he saw the movie *Holes* and he thought Shia was really good.

Extra activity

- Give students a few minutes to write some quiz questions about Shia LaBoeuf, e.g. *When was he born?* (6/11/86), etc.
- In pairs, students test each other and see how much they can remember about him.

Listening

Aim

To listen to and understand two teenagers discussing a movie

Background notes

- *Percy Jackson and the Lightning Thief* was released in 2010. The movie is about Percy Jackson, a teenager who is a descendant of a Greek god.
- *Tooth Fairy* was a movie released in 2010. It is a comedy about a hockey player who must spend one week as a tooth fairy. A tooth fairy gives children money or presents in exchange for a baby tooth that has fallen out.

Warm-up

- Ask students: *When did you go to the movies? What did you see? Did you talk about it with your friends?*

Exercise 3 1.35

- Give students time to read through the text and the answer choices before they listen.
- Play the CD. Students listen and choose the correct answers.
- Check the answers with the class.

ANSWERS / AUDIO CD TRACK 1.35

Sal Oh, hi Mike! How's it going?
Mike Not bad. And you?
Sal I'm great, thanks. Did you have a good weekend?
Mike Yes, actually, I did. I went out on Saturday. I went to the movies.
Sal Really? Did you go with Kate?
Mike No, I didn't. Kate didn't want to go because she was tired so I went with Kevin.
Sal And what movie did you see?
Mike Well Kevin wanted to see *Tooth Fairy* but I wanted to see *The Lightning Thief*. In the end, I won and we saw *The Lightning Thief*!
Sal What did Kevin think of the movie?
Mike I think he liked it.
Sal Did you like it, too?
Mike Yes, I loved it! The children were fantastic! They were incredible actors.

1 Saturday 2 Kate 3 she 4 Kevin 5 *The Lightning Thief* 6 quite liked 7 loved 8 fantastic

Extra activity

- Give students a few minutes to read the text with their correct answers.
- Books closed. Read out the text in exercise 3 sentence by sentence for students to write it down.
- Alternatively, you can ask for volunteers to write each sentence you dictate on the board.

Consolidation

- Encourage students to make a note of any new words and phrases in their vocabulary books.

Speaking

Aim

To ask and answer questions about movies

Warm-up

- Ask students about recent movies that they might have seen. Ask: *What did you think of them? Did you like them?* Offer your own opinion if you saw the movies.

Exercise 4

- Students think of a movie they saw last year and complete the chart with the information about it.
- Monitor and check that students are completing the information correctly and help as necessary.
- To help students, you can copy the chart onto the board and complete it with a movie of your own choice.

ANSWERS
Students' own answers.

Exercise 5 Pairwork

- In pairs, students ask and answer questions about the movies they watched.
- Remind them to use the question prompts, but encourage them to ask more questions and to add more details of their own if they can.
- Ask a student to ask you questions about your movie if you have completed the chart for yourself.
- Ask one or two pairs to feedback to the class on the movies they watched.
- Is there a class favorite?

ANSWERS
Students' own answers.

Extra activity

- Play *Charades* in small groups or as a whole class. Students think of a movie title and act it out for the group or the class. The others guess the name of the movie.

Writing

Aim

To write a short text about two movies

Background notes

- *Coraline* was a 2009 animated movie written by Neil Gaiman.
- *Astroboy* is a 2009 computer-animated movie, based loosely on the Japanese Manga character of Astroboy.
- *Night at the Museum* was a 2006 adventure-comedy movie based on a book. The story is set in New York City's Museum of Natural History. A second movie was released in 2009.

Warm-up

- Ask students to look at the movie posters and ask: *Do you know these movies? Did you see any of them? What did you think?*
- If you have seen the movies, offer your opinion.

Exercise 6

- Students write notes on each prompt, then they write a first draft of their text.
- Remind them to use the simple past and make sure they are using the regular and irregular forms correctly.
- Students swap drafts with a partner who corrects the errors.
- Students then write a final draft in class or for homework.
- Students can add photos or illustrations to their texts.
- Ask one or two students to tell the rest of the class about the movies they chose.

CD-ROM **WORKBOOK PAGE W25**

Grammar

Simple past: Regular and irregular (Affirmative, negative, interrogative, short answers)

Question words + Simple past

Vocabulary

Jobs

Movie types

Review B PAGES 46–47

Vocabulary

Exercise 1

ANSWERS

1 postal worker 2 doctor 3 lawyer 4 accountant
5 journalist 6 electrician 7 hairdresser 8 engineer
9 salesclerk

Exercise 2

ANSWERS

1 science fiction movie 2 fantasy movie 3 action movie
4 comedy 5 love story 6 horror movie

Grammar

Exercise 3

ANSWERS

1 stopped 2 thought 3 preferred 4 sang 5 did
6 stayed 7 watched 8 gave

Background notes

- The Golden Gate Bridge, City Hall, and Fisherman's Wharf are popular tourist attractions in San Francisco.
- Alcatraz Island is located in the San Francisco Bay. It is often called The Rock. The island has had many purposes over the years: a lighthouse, a military prison, and a federal prison until 1963. Nowadays it is a tourist attraction.
- Chinatown in San Francisco is one of the largest Chinese communities outside Asia. It is now a major tourist attraction.

Exercise 4

ANSWERS

1 was 2 saw 3 had 4 walked 5 bought 6 got
7 took 8 visited 9 tried 10 was

Exercise 5

ANSWERS

1 We didn't see *Land of the Lost* last night.
2 I didn't invite Marco to the party.
3 Lucy didn't spend a lot of money on vacation.
4 Abel didn't think the movie was good.
5 Mom didn't tell me to do my homework.

Exercise 6

ANSWERS

1 Did Ellen learn to play the piano at school? Yes, she did.
2 Did your parents meet after work? No, they didn't.
3 Did you see *Valentine's Day*? No, I didn't.
4 Did the postal worker deliver a letter for me? Yes, he / she did.
5 Did the electrician come this morning? No, he / she didn't.

Background notes

- *G.I. Joe* was a movie released in 2009. It is an action adventure science fiction comedy. It was inspired by a comic book called *G.I. Joe: A Real American Hero*.
- *Hannah Montana: The Movie* was a 2009 musical movie adaptation of the American teen sitcom *Hannah Montana*. It starred Miley Cyrus, Emily Osment, and Mitchel Musso.

Exercise 7

ANSWERS

1 didn't 2 Did she call 3 didn't 4 What did you do
5 Did you go 6 didn't 7 did you watch 8 I did
9 Did you like 10 I did 11 What did Natalia and Ruben think 12 Did she arrive 13 she didn't 14 What did she say 15 Did she apologize 16 she did

Got it?

Exercise 8

ANSWERS

1 traveled 2 waited 3 didn't sleep 4 started 5 went
6 said 7 told 8 asked 9 didn't know 10 was
11 didn't have 12 didn't do 13 didn't get 14 had

Exercise 9

ANSWERS

1 Did Sara travel to Hollywood? Yes, she did.
2 Who did she go with? She went with her mom and her friend Sophie.
3 Where did they wait all night? They waited outside the studio.
4 What time did the auditions start? They started at about nine o'clock.
5 Did Sara and Sophie know about the first audition? No, they didn't.
6 How did Sara do in her audition? She didn't do very well (because she was nervous).

Songs

The following songs would be appropriate to use at this point:

- *Cry me a river* by Justin Timberlake (simple past)
- *You're beautiful* by James Blunt (simple past)
- *I fought the war* by Sonny Curtis and the Crickets (simple past)
- *Sk8er boi* by Avril Lavigne (simple past)

Grammar

Simple past: Regular and irregular (Affirmative, negative, interrogative, short answers)

Question words + Simple past

Vocabulary

Movies

Topics

Media Studies: history of Walt Disney movies

Culture club B PAGE 48

Aims

To read and understand a text about the history of the Walt Disney company

Background notes

- The Walt Disney Company, see Unit 4, page 48.
- The Mickey Mouse Club was a long-running American TV show that began in 1955. It is produced by the Walt Disney Company.
- Britney Spears is an American singer and songwriter. She was born in 1981 in Mississippi. She has sold more than 83 million albums and earned more than $35 million in 2009.
- Justin Timberlake, see Unit 2, page 33.
- Christina Aguilera is an American singer songwriter who was born in 1980 in Staten Island, New York. Her fourth album was released in 2010 and she has earned more than $43 million.

Warm-up

- Ask students to look at the cartoon illustration and ask:
  Do you know this cartoon character? (Mickey Mouse)
  Did you watch him when you were younger? Which cartoon characters do you like?

Exercise 1

- In pairs or small groups, students do the quiz.
- They read the text quickly to check their answers.

ANSWERS

1 b 2 b 3 a 4 b 5 a

Exercise 2

- Students read the text again and complete the sentences.
- Remind them to look at the key words in each sentence and to think about the words they might be looking for, e.g. names, dates, etc.
- Students can compare answers in pairs.
- Check the answers with the class.

ANSWERS

1 *Plane Crazy*; 1928
2 it was a silent movie
3 started to talk
4 funny; clothes
5 a TV program; the *Mickey Mouse Club*
6 love Mickey Mouse

Exercise 3 Focus on you

- Students make notes on the questions on page 48 to prepare an oral presentation.
- They write a first draft of their presentation and swap with a partner who checks it for mistakes.
- Students write a final version.
- If students have access to a computer, they can do their presentation using PowerPoint.
- Ask students to give their presentations to the rest of the class.

ANSWERS

Students' own answers

Extra activity

- If students are interested in the topic, they can do more research for homework and write a short report to bring into class.

My progress PAGE 49

- For items 1–6, students read the sentences and complete the lists with their examples.
- If students have less than 3 / 5 for individual statements, encourage them to review the grammar or vocabulary and to do more practice.
- For items 7–10, students circle the answer which reflects the progress they have made in Units 3 and 4.
- If they have chosen *I'm not sure* or *No*, encourage them to review these sections and to do more practice.

Remember

Grammar
Simple present and present progressive
Possessive pronouns
Adverbs
Simple past: Regular and irregular

Vocabulary
Physical descriptions
Music
Jobs
Movies

Vocabulary PAGE 50

Aim

To review the vocabulary from Units 1–4

Exercise 1

ANSWERS

1 green eyes   2 classical guitarist   3 rock 'n' roll
4 postal worker   5 salesclerk   6 love story
7 horror movie

Exercise 2

ANSWERS

Students' own answers.

> **Extra activity**
> • Write more words for each category on the board for students to classify.
> • Ask stronger students to add as many words as they can to each category.

Grammar PAGES 50–51

Aim

To review the grammar from Units 1–4

Simple present and present progressive

Exercise 3

ANSWERS

1 1 Is she doing   2 isn't   3 never does   4 're watching
2 1 do you do   2 play   3 does your band play   4 aren't
   5 practice
3 1 do you like   2 don't like   3 read   4 are you reading
   5 'm reading   6 Does he write   7 doesn't   8 writes

> **Extra activity**
> • If students need further practice, copy one of the dialogues from exercise 3 onto the board.
> • Ask students to come out and write the verbs in the gaps in the correct form.

Possessive pronouns

Exercise 4

ANSWERS

1 Ours   2 yours   3 hers   4 Mine   5 theirs   6 hers

Adverbs

Exercise 5

ANSWERS

1 beautifully   2 well   3 badly   4 fast   5 quietly
6 fantastically

> **Extra activity**
> • In pairs or as a whole class, give students other adjectives for them to give you the adverbs.

Simple past

Exercise 6

ANSWERS

1 o   2 j   3 k   4 r   5 c   6 p   7 h   8 g   9 b   10 i
11 a   12 e   13 q   14 n   15 l   16 f   17 s   18 t   19 m
20 d

Exercise 7

ANSWERS

1 had   2 didn't go   3 didn't get up   4 got up   5 made
6 gave   7 spent   8 came   9 read   10 listened   11 went
12 were   13 ate   14 drank   15 had   16 saw   17 spoke
18 What did you do

5 Is Sam playing?

Grammar
Present progressive for future
Future time expressions
How long …? + take

Vocabulary
Transportation

Communication
Making arrangements

Skills
Reading: A magazine article about a skateboarder
Listening: An interview with a skateboarder
Speaking: Asking and answering questions about a future trip
Writing: An e-mail about a future trip

Topics
Society: Different ways to travel
Geography: Places around the world

Presentation PAGE 52

Aim
To present the new language in an interesting context

Story
Coach Carson is talking to some of the basketball team about their game on Saturday. He tells the players that Justin is the team captain. Sam arrives late to find out he isn't playing in the match because he did badly in his math test.

Warm-up
- Ask students to look at the photo. Ask: *Who can you see?* (Coach Carson, Teo, Alex, Joe, and Dylan) *Where are they?* (In the school gym) *What do you think they are they talking about?*

Exercise 1 Read and listen 1.36
- Give students time to read the answer options.
- Play the CD. Students read and listen and choose the correct answer.
- Students listen again and repeat.
- Go through the dialogue and the *Check it out!* box with the class.
- Play the CD again. Students listen and repeat chorally, then individually.

Transcript STUDENT BOOK PAGE 52

ANSWER
b Justin

Exercise 2 Comprehension
- Students read the dialogue again and complete Coach Carson's information sheet.
- Check the answers with the class.

ANSWERS
Meeting place: school **Transportation:** school bus
Departure time: two o'clock

Consolidation
- Remind students to make a note of any new words from the dialogue in their vocabulary books.

Language focus PAGE 53

Aim
To practice the target language in a new context

Exercise 3 Dialogue focus
- Students complete the dialogues.
- Students can compare answers in pairs. Do not check the answers at this point.

Exercise 4 1.37
- Play the CD. Students listen and check their answers.
- Students listen again and repeat chorally, then individually.

ANSWERS / AUDIO CD TRACK 1.37
1 **Joe** Where are we meeting?
   CC [1]We're meeting at the school at one thirty.
2 **Dylan** [2]How are we getting to Riverfield?
   CC [3]We're taking the school bus.
3 **Adam** [4]What time is it leaving?
   CC [5]It's leaving at two o'clock sharp.
4 **Teo** [6]Is Sam playing?
   CC [7]No, he isn't. Justin is taking his place.

Exercise 5 Focus on you
- Students read the example dialogue and write three more dialogues using the information on page 53.
- Monitor and check that students are using the present continuous correctly. Make a note of any repeated errors to go over at the end of the lesson.

ANSWERS
Students' own answers.

Exercise 6 Pairwork
- In pairs, students practice their dialogues from exercise 5.
- Monitor and check.
- Ask one or two pairs to act out their dialogues in front of the class.

ANSWERS
Students' own answers.

Vocabulary PAGE 54

Transportation

Aim

To present and practice transportation vocabulary: *airplane, bike, boat, bus, car, ferry, helicopter, motorcycle, subway, taxi, train, truck*

Warm-up

* Ask students one or two questions about transportation, e.g. *How do you get to school? Do you travel by bus? Do you walk? Do your parents have a car?*, and elicit as many different forms of transport as possible. Write them on the board.

Exercise 1

* Students match the pictures with the kinds of transportation.
* Students can compare answers with a partner.
* Do not check the answers at this point.

Exercise 2 🔊 1.38

* Play the CD. Students listen and check their answers to exercise 1.
* Students listen again and repeat chorally, then individually.
* Draw students' attention to the *Look!* box and go through it with the class.
* Ask students to give you another example of *by* with a form of transportation from exercise 1, e.g. *by boat*.

ANSWERS / AUDIO CD TRACK 1.38

1 car   2 airplane   3 ferry   4 helicopter   5 subway
6 bus   7 train   8 boat   9 taxi   10 truck   11 bike
12 motorcycle

Extra activity

* Give students a few minutes to look at the pictures in exercise 1 again.
* Books closed. In pairs or as a whole class, call out the number of a picture for students to give you the type of transport, e.g. T: *6* SS: *bus*, etc.

Extra activity

* In pairs or as a whole class, students draw a form of transportation for the others to guess what it is before they have finished drawing. The student who guesses correctly has the next turn.

Exercise 3 Pairwork

* In pairs, students ask and answer questions about how they and their family go to work or school.
* If students need more support, go through the example dialogue with them, drawing their attention to the questions and answers and the use of adverbs of frequency.
* Monitor and check that students are taking turns to ask and answer questions and that they are using the vocabulary correctly. Make a note of any repeated errors to go over at the end of the lesson.
* Ask one or two pairs to act out their dialogues for the class.

ANSWERS
Students' own answers.

Extra activity

* In pairs or groups, students say which kinds of transportation they *often*, *sometimes*, *rarely* or *never* use. Which kinds of transportation are the most / least popular?

Consolidation

* Remind students to make a note of the vocabulary from this lesson in their vocabulary books. Encourage them to add illustrations or translations to help them remember it.

CD-ROM   WORKBOOK PAGE W28

Grammar PAGE 55

Present progressive for future

Aim

To present and practice the present progressive for future use

Warm-up

- Ask students one or two questions about the dialogue on page 52 to elicit present progressive for future use, e.g. *When is the basketball match?* (It's on Saturday) *Where is the basketball team meeting?* (They're meeting at the school).
- Alternatively, ask students questions about their plans for the weekend, e.g. *What are you doing on the weekend? Where are you going? Who are you going with? How are you getting there?*, etc.

Think! box

- Go through the *Think!* box with the class. Draw students' attention to the rules and expressions.
- Ask students to look back at the dialogue on page 52 and find examples of this tense.
- Students complete the rule.
- Check the answers with the class.

> **ANSWER**
> future plans

Rules PAGE W26

Aim

To present and practice time expressions

Future time expressions

- Go through the grammar chart with the class and draw students' attention to the different ways of expressing future time. Elicit or explain that if we use the present progressive to talk about the future, we must use a future time expression.
- Review how to form the present progressive at this point if necessary. Ask one or two present progressive future questions to make sure students understand, e.g. T: *What are you doing tomorrow evening, Juli?* SS: *I'm going to the movies.*
- Direct students to the rules on page W26 if necessary.

Rules PAGE W26

Exercise 1

- Students look at Robert's dayplanner and rewrite the sentences with true information.
- Students can compare answers in pairs.
- Check the answers with the class.

> **ANSWERS**
> 1 He isn't having a piano lesson on Tuesday. He's playing tennis with Alison.
> 2 He isn't visiting his grandparents on Wednesday evening. He's visiting his grandparents on Wednesday afternoon.
> 3 He isn't starting his history project on Thursday. He's finishing his science project.

4 He isn't staying at home on Friday evening. He's having pizza with Ben and Jake.
5 He isn't playing basketball on Saturday. He's watching the baseball game at John's house.
6 He isn't going swimming with Seb on Sunday. He's going skateboarding with Seb.

> **Extra activity**
> - If students need more practice, call out future time expressions from the chart for students to give you the preceding word, e.g. T: *Tuesday* SS: *on*, etc.

Exercise 2

- Students complete the dayplanner with their own information and then write sentences.
- Remind them to refer back to exercise 1 if necessary.
- Ask one or two students to read out their sentences to the class. Monitor for accurate use of the present progressive and future time expressions and review as necessary.

> **ANSWERS**
> Students' own answers.

Exercise 3

- Students read the sentences and choose the correct answers.
- Remind them to refer back to the grammar charts if necessary.
- Check the answers with the class.

> **ANSWERS**
> 1 evening   2 afternoon   3 Monday   4 October 5th
> 5 evening   6 tomorrow

Finished?

- In pairs, students choose five future time expressions and say what their plans are.
- Ask one or two pairs to tell the rest of the class about their plans.

> **ANSWERS**
> Students' own answers.

> **Extra activity**
> - In small groups or as a whole class, one student thinks of an activity they are doing on the weekend and acts it out. The others guess what the student is doing, e.g.
> S1: *Are you going skateboarding?* S2: *No, I'm not.*
> S3: *Are you playing chess?*, etc.

> **Consolidation**
> - Remind students to make a note of the grammar rules and examples from this lesson in their grammar books.

CD-ROM WORKBOOK PAGES W28–W29

Communication PAGE 56

Making arrangements

Aim

To present and practice the language for making arrangements

Warm-up

- Ask students how they make arrangements with their friends, e.g. *Do you call them on their cell phones, send a text, or discuss it at school?*
- Ask them what is the most important thing for them when they make an arrangement, e.g. what they are doing, where they are going, or when they are going.

Exercise 1 🔊 1.39

- Give students time to read the answer choices before they listen.
- Play the CD. Students read and listen and choose the correct answers.
- Students can compare answers in pairs.
- Play the CD. Students listen and check their answers.
- Students listen again and repeat chorally, then individually.

ANSWERS / AUDIO CD TRACK 1.39

Sarah Hi, Olivia. Are you free tomorrow evening?
Olivia No, I'm not. I'm seeing Kate tomorrow, but I'm free on Tuesday evening.
Sarah Great. Let's do something together on Tuesday then.
Olivia Good idea. What do you want to do?
Sarah How about ¹going to the movies?
Olivia There aren't any good movies on at the moment. Why don't we ²go bowling instead?
Sarah That's a great idea. Let's meet in front of ³my house.
Olivia OK. At what time? How long does it take to get there?
Sarah It takes about ⁴30 minutes. Is ⁵seven thirty OK?
Olivia Yes, that's fine. See you then.

1 going to the movies   2 go bowling   3 my house   4 30
5 seven

- Go through the *You say, You answer* box with the class. Draw students' attention to the different ways of asking and answering to make arrangements.
- Refer them back to the dialogue to find and underline the phrases Sarah and Olivia used.

Exercise 2 Pronunciation 🔊 1.40

- Read through the sentences as a class before students listen.
- Play the CD. Students listen and repeat chorally, then individually.

Transcript STUDENT BOOK PAGE 56

> ### Extra activity
> - If students need more practice, repeat each sentence from the end, one word at a time, e.g. *swimming, go swimming, Let's go swimming* for students to repeat chorally.

Exercise 3 🔊 1.41

- Give students time to read the questions before they listen.
- Play the CD. Students listen and answer the questions.
- Check the answers with the class.

ANSWERS / AUDIO CD TRACK 1.41

1 **Fred** Why don't we watch a DVD this evening?
  Si No, I want to go out. Let's go bowling.
  Fred OK. Let's meet in front of the teen center.
  Si At what time?
  Fred Let's meet at seven forty-five.
  Si Great. See you then.
2 **Nic** Are you free this weekend?
  Ellie Yes, I am.
  Nic Great! Let's go shopping!
  Ellie No, I can't. I don't have any money!
  Nic OK. Why don't you come to my house and watch a DVD? I have the new James Bond movie.
  Ellie That's a great idea. At what time?
  Nic Is seven thirty OK?
  Ellie Fine. See you at seven thirty.
3 **Jack** Hi Dan. It's Jack. What are you doing this afternoon?
  Dan Hi Jack. I'm watching a DVD, but it isn't very good.
  Jack Let's go out then.
  Dan Good idea.
  Jack How about going to the swimming pool?
  Dan No, I can't swim. How about going skateboarding?
  Jack That sounds great. Where shall we meet?
  Dan Let's meet at the skate park at three thirty.
  Jack All right. See you then.

1 **Place:** They're meeting in front of / at the teen center.
  Time: They're meeting at 7:45.
2 **Activity:** They're watching a DVD.
  Place: They're meeting at the first speaker's house.
  Time: They're meeting at 7:30.
3 **Activity:** They're going skateboarding.
  Place: They're meeting at the skate park.
  Time: They're meeting at 3:30.

Exercise 4 Pairwork

- In pairs, students make arrangements and accept or refuse suggestions using the ideas in the box.
- Stronger students can use their own ideas if they prefer.
- Monitor and check that students are using the questions and answers for making arrangements correctly. Make a note of any repeated errors to go over at the end of the lesson.
- Ask one or two pairs to act out their dialogues for the rest of the class.

ANSWERS

Students' own answers.

> ## Consolidation
> - Remind students to make a note of the language for making arrangements in their vocabulary books.

CD-ROM WORKBOOK PAGE W30

Grammar PAGE 57

How long …? + take

Aim

To present and practice *How long …? + take*

Warm-up

- Ask students: *How do you get to school? Is it far from your house to school?* and elicit responses.

Think! box

- Go through the *Think!* box with the class and draw students' attention to the use of the question to ask about length of time, and the use of *it* instead of a subject pronoun. Highlight the fact that the answer contains a time expression.
- Direct students back to the dialogue on page 52 to find an example of this expression.
- Students complete the rule.
- Check the answers with the class and refer students to the rules on page W27 if necessary.

ANSWERS

1 How long   **2** take   **3** takes

Rules PAGE W27

Background notes

- Los Angeles, see Unit 1, page 26.
- San Francisco is in the state of California on the west coast of the U.S. and is a popular tourist destination. Its famous landmarks include the Golden Gate Bridge, the former prison Alcatraz, and its cable cars.
- Miami is a major city in the U.S. on the Atlantic coast in south-east Florida. The port in Miami is the world's largest cruise ship port. Miami is the headquarters for the Latin American part of multinational businesses, including Disney, Microsoft, and Sony.
- Atlanta is the capital of the state of Georgia. It is an important city for businesses and transportation. Coca-Cola has its headquarters there.
- The Statue of Liberty, see Unit 1, page 26.

Exercise 1

- Students write questions and answers.
- Remind them to refer back to the grammar chart if necessary.
- Students can compare answers in pairs.
- Check the answers with the class.

ANSWERS

1 How long does it take to fly from Miami to Atlanta?
 It takes two hours.
2 How long does it take you to have breakfast?
 It takes 15 minutes.
3 How long does it take to go to the Statue of Liberty by ferry?
 It takes 1 hour.
4 How long does it take you to take a shower?
 It takes 5 minutes.

5 How long does it take you to do your homework?
 It takes 2 hours.
6 How long does it take you to go to school?
 It takes 20 minutes.

Extra activity

- Students can answer questions 2, 4, 5, and 6 for themselves. They can compare answers with a partner.

Background notes

- Boston is the capital and the largest city in the state of New England.
- New Haven is in the state of Connecticut in the south central part of the U.S. Yale University is in New Haven.
- Fenway district is a historic district in Boston, Massachussets.
- Belo Horizonte is the capital of the state of Minas Gerais in south-east Brazil.

Exercise 2

- Students complete the e-mail with the correct forms of the verbs in the box.
- Remind them to refer back to the grammar boxes in the unit if necessary.
- Check the answers with the class.

ANSWERS

1 'm going / 'm traveling   **2** 're taking   **3** 're meeting   **4** 're going   **5** 're having   **6** are watching   **7** 're organizing   **8** are coming   **9** are (you) doing   **10** travel / go

Exercise 3 Game!

- Students make plans for a vacation using as many words as they can from the chart.
- If students need more support, go through the chart and the example with them before they start.
- In pairs, students make their plans and exchange information.
- Monitor and check that they are using the present progressive for future, transportation phrases, and *it takes* correctly.
- Ask one or two pairs to tell the rest of the class about their plans.

ANSWERS
Students' own answers.

Finished?

- Students write five questions with *How long does it take you …?* for their partner to answer.
- Students ask their partner their questions.

ANSWERS
Students' own answers.

Consolidation

- Remind students to make a note of the grammar rules and examples from the lesson in their grammar books.

CD-ROM WORKBOOK PAGE W29

Skills PAGES 58–59

Reading

Aim

To read and understand a magazine text about a skateboarder

Background notes

- Australia is a country in the southern hemisphere. It became a Commonwealth state in 1901, and Canberra is the capital city.
- Perth is a city in the western part of Australia, which was founded in 1829.
- Brisbane is the largest city in the Australian state of Queensland, which is situated on the east coast of the country.
- The emu is the largest native Australian bird. It can travel long distances very quickly, but it cannot fly.

Warm-up

- Ask students what they know about Australia and elicit any facts. If you have a map of Australia you can put it on the board and discuss it with students.
- Ask them to look at the photo of David Cornthwaite and to discuss what they think he did.

Exercise 1

- Before students read the text in detail, ask questions about the text, e.g. *Who is David?* (a skateboarder) *What did he do?* (travel across Australia) *How many different types of transportation are there in the text?* (four: skateboard, bike, jeep, truck).
- Students skim the text to find the answers to your questions.
- Students read the text in detail and answer the questions.
- Remind them to look at the questions carefully and to think about the information they will need for the answers, e.g. numbers, distances, etc.
- Students can compare answers in pairs.
- Check the answers with the class.

ANSWERS
1 He skated about 50 kilometers every day.
2 Seven people traveled with him.
3 He met some snakes, lots of dogs, and an emu.
4 He used 13 pairs of shoes.
5 He made $80,000 for charity.

Extra activity
- Ask students to find adjectives in the text with the opposite meanings: *cold* (hot), *tiny* (enormous), *safe* (dangerous), *small* (big), *slow* (fast), *young* (old).

Listening

Aim

To listen to and understand an interview with a skateboarder

Warm-up

- Ask students what they think Greg will talk about in his interview and elicit one or two ideas.

Exercise 2   1.42

- Give students time to read the questions before they listen and encourage them to think about the key words.
- Play the CD. Students listen and decide if the statements are true or false.
- Check the answers with the class.
- Students listen again and correct the false statements. Encourage them to listen carefully for the information they need to correct the false statements.
- Check the answers with the class.
- You can write the statements on the board and ask volunteers to come out and correct the false ones.

ANSWERS / AUDIO CD TRACK 1.42

Interviewer	Greg Fisher is a champion skateboarder and [1]he's skateboarding across the U.S. this summer. Welcome to the program, Greg.
Greg	Thanks. It's great to be here.
Interviewer	When are you leaving, Greg?
Greg	I'm leaving from New Port, Oregon, on [2]June twelfth.
Interviewer	Who are you traveling with?
Greg	[3]My two crazy friends Adam and Zac. They're driving a school bus behind me.
Interviewer	A school bus?
Greg	Yes, [4]we're sleeping in a big yellow school bus! It has three beds, a refrigerator, and a TV!
Interviewer	Cool! So, where are you going first?
Greg	[5]First, we're going to San Francisco, California.
Interviewer	What other states are you traveling through?
Greg	We're traveling through Nevada, Utah, and Colorado.
Interviewer	What's your final destination?
Greg	Our final destination is the east coast. [6]We want to get to Springfield, Virginia.
Interviewer	When are you hoping to get there?
Greg	I'm hoping to get there [7]at the end of August.
Interviewer	Why are you doing this, Greg?
Greg	[8]I'm collecting money for charity.
Interviewer	Well, good luck!

1 False. He's skateboarding across the U.S.   2 True.   3 False. He's traveling with his friends Adam and Zac.   4 True.
5 False. He's going to San Francisco, California first.   6 True.
7 False. He's hoping to get to the east coast at the end of August.   8 True.

Extra activity
- In pairs or as a whole class, students mark Greg's route on a map of the U.S.
- You can put a map on the board and ask for volunteers to come out and mark each stage of his route.

Speaking

Aim

To ask and answer questions about a future trip

Background notes

- San Diego is the second largest city in California. It is located on the Pacific Ocean on the west coast of the U.S.
- The California Tower is a 60m tower and a popular tourist attraction in Balboa Park in San Diego.
- Balboa Park is an urban park in San Diego. The park has open areas but it also has museums, theaters, places to eat, and shops. The San Diego Zoo is also inside the park.
- Sea World is a popular tourist attraction in San Diego. There are aquariums, animal shows, and water rides.

Warm-up

- Ask students if they have made any trips recently with their family or with school for sports games or field trips. If so, ask them a few questions, e.g. *Where did you go? Who did you go with? What did you do? How did you get there?*
- Ask students to look at the photo and ask: *Do you know where it is?* (San Diego) *Have you ever been there?*

Exercise 3 Pairwork

- Students work alone and complete the factfile with the missing information.
- If students need more support, go through the example and each item with them and elicit ideas.
- Students work in pairs. They take it in turns to ask and answer questions about the trip they are planning.
- Monitor and check that students are taking turns to ask and answer questions and that they are using the present progressive, *how long* and *take*, and transportation words correctly. Make a note of any repeated errors to go over at the end of the lesson.
- Ask one or two pairs to act out their dialogues for the rest of the class.

ANSWERS
Students' own answers.

> ### Extra activity
> - In pairs, students discuss if they would like to visit San Diego and what they would do.
> - Ask pairs to report back to the class.

Writing

Aim

To write an e-mail about a trip you are planning

Warm-up

- Ask students what they usually write when they start and finish an e-mail to a friend.
- Draw their attention to the opening and closing lines of the e-mail to show an example of each in English. Ask them if they know any other ways of starting and finishing an e-mail in English and elicit or give some examples, e.g. *Hello, Bye for now, Best wishes, Be in touch again soon,* etc.

Exercise 4

- Students complete the e-mail with the information from exercise 3.
- Remind them to read the e-mail through first and to think about the words before and after each gap to help them work out what to write.
- Check the answers with the class.

ANSWERS
1 students' own answer   2 're leaving
3 students' own answer   4 a hotel near the California Tower
5 're visiting   6 're spending   7 're taking

Exercise 5

- Students imagine they are planning a trip and write an e-mail to a friend about their plans. Students can choose a place they know well or they can find out some facts about a place of their choice.
- Remind them to refer back to the questions in exercise 3 and to make notes on each one.
- Students write a rough draft of their e-mail, using their notes.
- They swap drafts with a partner who corrects the mistakes.
- Remind them to use appropriate opening and closing phrases (see *Warm-up*).
- Students write a final draft in the class or for homework.

ANSWERS
Students' own answers.

> ### Extra activity
> - Students can read out their e-mails to the rest of the class. Is there a favorite place?

> ### Consolidation
> - Remind students to make a note of any new words or phrases from this lesson in their vocabulary books.

CD-ROM WORKBOOK PAGE W31

6 Are there any tomatoes?

Grammar
Countable / Uncountable nouns
some / any
a lot of / much / many
How much …? / How many …?
a little / a few

Vocabulary
Food and drink

Communication
Ordering food and drink

Skills
Reading: A text about a young cook
Listening: Two teenagers talking about the food they eat
Speaking: Talking about the food you like
Writing: A short text about your diet

Topics
Multiculturalism: Food around the world
Health and diet

Presentation PAGE 60

Aim
To present the new language in a motivating context

Story
Teo, Zoe, and Sam are in the kitchen. Teo is looking in the refrigerator with Zoe for something to eat. Sam says he doesn't want anything to eat. Teo explains to Zoe it is because he got a bad mark in a math test and is off the basketball team. Zoe offers to help Sam with his studying.

Warm-up
- Ask students to look at the photo. Ask: *Who can you see?* (Zoe, Teo, and Sam) *Where are they?* (in the kitchen) *How do you think Sam feels?* (he feels sad)

Exercise 1 Read and listen 1.43
- Students read the answer choices before they listen.
- Play the CD. Students read and listen and choose the correct answer.
- Check the answer with the class.
- Go through the dialogue and the *Check it out!* box.
- Play the CD again. Students listen and repeat chorally, then individually.

Transcript STUDENT BOOK PAGE 60

ANSWER
b sandwiches

Exercise 2 Comprehension
- Students answer the questions individually.
- Check the answers with the class. Ask students to read out their full answers.

ANSWERS
1 Zoe offers Teo a ham sandwich.
2 Sam isn't hungry because he got a bad mark in the math test.
3 She offers to help him study.

> ### Consolidation
> - Remind students to make a note of any new vocabulary from the dialogue in their vocabulary books.

Language focus PAGE 61

Aim
To practice the target language in a new context

Exercise 3 Dialogue focus
- Students read the sentences and put them in the correct order. Remind them to use the dialogue in exercise 1 to help them. Do not check the answers at this point.

Exercise 4 1.44
- Play the CD. Students listen and check their answers.
- Students listen again and repeat chorally, then individually.

ANSWERS / AUDIO CD TRACK 1.44
1 **Teo** I'm hungry. Is there any food in the refrigerator, Zoe?
  Zoe I don't know. Let me see. Yes, there is, ¹but there isn't much. There's some ham. ²Would you like a ham sandwich?
  Teo Yes, OK.
2 **Teo** ³Are there any tomatoes?
  Zoe No, there aren't. ⁴There's a lot of lettuce.
  Teo Yuck! I hate lettuce. ⁵Is there any cheese?
  Zoe No, there isn't. ⁶There are some carrots, but there aren't many.
3 **Zoe** ⁷Anyway, how many ham sandwiches do you want?
  Teo Just a couple. ⁸What about you, Sam?
  Sam ⁹No, not for me, thanks. I'm not hungry.

Exercise 5 Focus on you
- In groups of three, students write their own dialogues using the food in the box.

ANSWERS
Students' own answers.

Exercise 6 Group work
- In groups of three, students practice their dialogues.
- Students can work in a different group if they prefer.
- Ask one or two groups to act out their dialogues.

ANSWERS
Students' own answers.

Vocabulary PAGE 62

Food and drink

Aim

To present and practice vocabulary for food and drink: *apple, beef, bread, carrot, cheese, chicken, cookie, egg, mango, milk, orange juice, potato, rice, salmon, tomato, tuna, water, yogurt*

Warm-up

- Ask students: *What do you eat and drink for breakfast?* Elicit food and drink items and write them on the board.

Exercise 1

- Individually or in pairs, students match the words with the pictures.
- Do not check the answers at this point.

Exercise 2 🔊 1.45

- Play the CD. Students listen and check their answers to exercise 1.
- Students listen again and repeat chorally, then individually.
- Go through the *Look!* box with the class and draw students' attention to the animals and the meat they produce.
- Ask them if this is similar or different in their own language.

ANSWERS / AUDIO CD TRACK 1.45

1 tuna   2 chicken   3 potato   4 apple   5 cheese
6 bread   7 milk   8 salmon   9 beef   10 tomato   11 rice
12 yogurt   13 cookie   14 water   15 carrot   16 mango
17 egg   18 orange juice

Extra activity 1

- Give students a few minutes to look at the food pictures in exercise 1.
- Books closed. Call out a number of a picture for students to give you the name of the food or drink.

Extra activity 2

- As a whole class or in pairs, students play *Hangman* with the food and drink vocabulary.

Exercise 3

- Students copy and complete the chart with food words from exercise 1.
- Encourage them to add any more food words they know.
- Students can compare charts in pairs.
- Check the answers with the class. You can copy the chart onto the board and ask students to come out and complete it.

ANSWERS
Fruit: apple, mango, tomato (note: some students may prefer to include *tomato* as a vegetable)
Vegetables: carrot, potato
Meat: beef, chicken, duck, ham, lamb, mutton, pork
Fish: salmon, tuna
Dairy products: cheese, milk, yogurt, egg
Drinks: milk, orange juice, water

Exercise 4 Pairwork

- In pairs, students talk about the food and drinks they like and don't like.
- Ask a pair of students to read out the example dialogue and draw students' attention to the questions and the verbs to use.
- Monitor and check that students are taking turns to ask and answer questions.
- Ask one or two pairs to act out their dialogues for the rest of the class.

ANSWERS
Students' own answers.

Extra activity

- Play a memory game. In small groups or as a whole class, students imagine they went shopping and bought food and drink. Students must say a food or drink item and remember what the person before them said, e.g. S1: *I went shopping and I bought a mango.* S2: *I went shopping and I bought a mango and a cookie,* etc.

Consolidation

- Remind students to make a note of the new vocabulary from this lesson in their vocabulary books. Encourage them to draw pictures, write a translation, or classify the words if it helps them to remember the vocabulary more easily.

CD-ROM   WORKBOOK PAGE W34

Grammar PAGE 63

Countable / Uncountable nouns

Aim

To present and practice countable and uncountable nouns

Warm-up

- Draw one or two countable and uncountable food items on the board, e.g. three apples, a piece of cheese.
- Ask students: *How many apples are there?* and elicit the answer (three). Ask: *Can you count the apples?* and elicit the answer (yes). Repeat the procedure for the cheese and establish that the cheese cannot be counted.

Grammar chart / Think! box

- Go through the grammar chart as a class, drawing students' attention to the fact that we can count some items in English, but not others.
- Explain that countable nouns can be singular or plural, we use *a / an* with singular countable nouns in affirmative and negative sentences, and uncountable nouns can only be singular.
- Ask students to look back at the dialogue on page 60 and find examples of countable and uncountable nouns.
- Students read and complete the rules in the *Think!* box.
- Check the answers with the class and remind students to check the rules on page W32.

ANSWERS
1 singular   2 plural   3 singular

Rules PAGE W32

Exercise 1

- Students complete the chart with five words from page 62 in each category.
- Check the answers with the class. You can copy the chart onto the board and ask students to come out and complete it with their answers.
- Draw students' attention to any changes in spelling from singular to plural, e.g. *potatoes, tomatoes*.

ANSWERS
Countable, Singular: (five of the following) a potato, an apple, a tomato, a cookie, a carrot, a mango
Countable, Plural: (five of the following) potatoes, apples, tomatoes, cookies, carrots, mangoes
Uncountable, Singular only: (five of the following) tuna, chicken, cheese, bread, salmon, rice, yogurt, water, orange juice, beef

some / any

Aim

To present and practice *some / any*

Grammar chart / Think! box

- Go through the grammar chart with the class.
- Ask students to look back at the dialogue on page 60 and find examples of *some* and *any*.
- Students read the *Think!* box and complete the rules.

- Check the answers with the class and remind students to check the rules on page W32.

ANSWERS
1 some   2 any

Rules PAGE W32

Exercise 2

- Students read the sentences and choose the correct answers.
- Remind them to refer back to the grammar chart if necessary.
- Check the answers with the class.

ANSWERS
1 any   2 any   3 some   4 any   5 some

a lot of / much / many

Aim

To present and practice *a lot of / much / many*

Grammar chart / Think! box

- Go through the grammar chart as a class. Elicit or explain when we use *a lot of*. We use *a lot of* in affirmative sentences with plural countable and uncountable nouns.
- Ask students to look back at the dialogue on page 60 to find more examples of *a lot of*, *much* and *many*.
- Students read the *Think!* box and choose the correct options.
- Check the answers with the class. Remind students to check the rules on page W32 if necessary.

ANSWERS
1 countable   2 uncountable

Rules PAGE W32

Exercise 3

- Students complete the sentences with *a lot of, much*, and *many*.
- Check the answers with the class.

ANSWERS
1 a lot of   2 many   3 many   4 a lot of   5 many
6 much

Exercise 4 Game!

- In pairs, students play a guessing game.
- Each student writes down six items of food they have in their refrigerator at home. They ask and answer questions to guess what the items are.
- Monitor and check that students are taking turns to ask and answer questions and that they are using the correct question and answer forms.
- The pair who guesses all the items correctly in the quickest time, is the winner.

> ### Consolidation
> - Remind students to make a note of the grammar rules and examples from this lesson in their grammar books. Encourage them to write translations or examples of their own to help them remember it.

CD-ROM WORKBOOK PAGE W34

Communication PAGE 64

Ordering food and drink

Aim

To present and practice the language for ordering food and drink

Warm-up

- Ask students: *Do you go out to eat with your family or friends? Where do you go? What do you like to eat and drink?* Elicit their replies.

Exercise 1 1.46

- Give students time to read through the dialogue and the words in the box before they listen.
- Play the CD. Students listen and complete the dialogue.
- Stronger students can read and complete the dialogue without listening.
- Students can compare answers in pairs.
- Play the CD. Students listen and check their answers.
- Students listen again and repeat chorally, then individually.

ANSWERS / AUDIO CD TRACK 1.46

Server	How can I help you?
Mark	I'd like a <u>chicken</u> sandwich, please.
Server	OK. What would you like to drink?
Mark	I'll have a [1]<u>soda</u>.
Server	Large or small?
Mark	Large, please.
Server	OK. And what about you? What would you like to eat?
Susan	I'd like a baked [2]<u>potato</u> with [3]<u>tuna</u>.
Server	OK. Would you like a drink?
Susan	Yes, please. I'll have an [4]<u>orange juice</u> and I'd like a few [5]<u>cookies</u>, too.
Server	OK. That's $15.75.

1 soda **2** potato **3** tuna **4** orange juice **5** cookies

- Go through the *You ask, You answer* box with the class. Ask students to look back at the dialogue and to find the expressions in the box.
- Ask one or two stronger students to ask and answer using the expressions in the box.

Exercise 2 Pronunciation 1.47

- Play the CD. Students listen and repeat chorally, then individually.
- Write the words *would you* on the board and ask students what they notice about the pronunciation of them in the questions. Elicit or explain that we shorten the sounds and so it sounds like /wədʒə/.

Transcript STUDENT BOOK PAGE 64

Extra activity

- If you feel students need more practice with this area, read each question from the end, word by word, for students to repeat chorally, e.g. *eat?, to eat?, like to eat?, you like to eat?, would you like to eat?, What would you like to eat?*
- Encourage students to think about intonation in questions.

Exercise 3 1.48

- Give students time to read the chart.
- Play the CD. Students listen and complete the chart.
- Students can compare answers in pairs. Play the CD again if necessary. Do not check the answers at this point.

Exercise 4 1.48

- Play the CD. Students listen and check their answers to exercise 3.

ANSWERS / AUDIO CD TRACK 1.48

1	**Server**	What would you like to eat?
	Man	I'll have a baked potato with cheese, please.
	Server	Would you like a drink?
	Man	Yes, please. I'd like a glass of orange juice.
2	**Server**	What would you like to eat?
	Boy	I'd like a burger and fries, please.
	Server	Would you like a drink?
	Boy	No, thank you.
3	**Server**	What would you like to eat?
	Girl	I'll have an egg and tomato sandwich, please.
	Server	Would you like a drink?
	Girl	Yes, please. I'd like a glass of water.

1 Food: baked potato with cheese **Drink:** glass of orange juice

2 Food: burger and fries No drink

3 Food: egg and tomato sandwich **Drink:** a glass of water

Extra activity

- In groups of three, students act out one of the dialogues from exercise 3. Encourage them to use the expressions from the *You ask, You answer* box.

Exercise 5 Group work

- In groups of three, students look at the menu and order food and drinks.
- Monitor and check that students are taking turns to ask and answer questions and that they are using the correct question and answer forms.

ANSWERS

Students' own answers.

Extra activity

- Prices quiz. In pairs or as a whole class, give students some combinations of things from the menu for them to give you the total price, e.g. T: *a cheese sandwich and a small soda* SS: *$5.80*

Consolidation

- Remind students to make a note of any new words and expressions from the lesson in their vocabulary books.

CD-ROM WORKBOOK PAGE W34

Grammar PAGE 65

How much …? / How many …?

Aim

To present and practice questions with *How much …? / How many …?*

Warm-up

- Draw one or two countable and uncountable food items on the board, e.g. lots of bread and apples, and ask students: *How many apples are there? How much bread is there?*

Grammar chart / Think! box

- Go through the grammar chart with the class.
- Ask students to look back at the dialogue on page 60 and find some examples.
- Students read the *Think!* box and complete the rules.
- Check the answers with the class and remind students to check the rules on page W33.

ANSWERS

1 how many   2 how much

Rules PAGE W33

Exercise 1

- Students read the recipe and complete the questions with *How much* or *How many*.
- Remind them to look at the noun after the gap and to work out if it is countable or uncountable.
- Check the answers with the class before students answer the questions.
- Students then write the answers to the questions.
- Check the answers with the class.

ANSWERS

1 <u>How many</u> strawberries are there?
   There are 12 large strawberries.
2 <u>How much</u> strawberry ice cream is there?
   There are 100 grams of strawberry ice cream.
3 <u>How many</u> oranges are there?
   There is one orange.
4 <u>How many</u> people is the recipe for?
   The recipe is for four people.

Extra activity

- Ask students to think about their favorite recipe.
- Students write out the recipe.
- In pairs, students ask and answer questions about the ingredients, like those in exercise 1.

---

a little / a few

Aim

To present and practice *a little / a few*

Warm-up

- Draw one or two more food items on the board, e.g. a bowl with a little ice cream, a few oranges. Ask: *How much ice*

cream is there? How many oranges are there? and elicit or give the answers: *There's a little ice cream. There are a few oranges.*

Think! box

- Students read the *Think!* box and then choose the correct word.
- Check the answers with the class, making sure that students know we use *a little* with countable nouns, and *a few* with plural countable nouns. Elicit or explain that *a little* is the same as *not much* and *a few* is the same as *not many*.
- Remind them to check the rules on page W33.

ANSWERS

1 uncountable   2 countable

Rules PAGE W33

Exercise 2

- Students complete the sentences with *a little* or *a few*.
- Remind them to look at the noun after each gap to help them work out which words to use.
- Check the answers with the class.

ANSWERS

1 a little   2 a few   3 a little   4 a few   5 a little   6 a few
7 a little   8 a few

Extra activity

- If you feel students need more practice with this area, call out some nouns for students to say *a little* or *a few*, e.g. T: *books* SS: *a few*, etc.

Exercise 3

- Students read the dialogue and choose the correct answers.
- Students can compare answers in pairs.
- Check the answers with the class.

ANSWERS

1 some   2 How much   3 much   4 some
5 How much   6 a lot of   7 a little   8 a lot of   9 any
10 some   11 some   12 a few   13 a few

Finished?

- Students write questions with *How much …?* and *How many…?* to ask you.
- Give students the opportunity to ask you questions at the end of the lesson and answer them as honestly as you can!

ANSWERS

Students' own questions.

Consolidation

- Encourage students to make a note of the grammar rules and examples from this lesson in their grammar books. Remind them to write translations or their own examples if it will help them remember more easily.

CD-ROM **WORKBOOK PAGE W35**

Skills PAGES 66–67

Reading

Aim

To read and understand a magazine article about a young cook

Warm-up

- Ask students: *What is your favorite food? Do you cook at home? Do you think you have a healthy diet?*
- Ask students to look at the photo and ask: *Do you know who this is? What is he doing?*

Exercise 1

- Before students read the text for details, ask them to skim it quickly and to find out how many cook books Sam Stern has written (five).
- Ask students to read the topics (a–d) and then to read the text and match the topics with the paragraphs.
- Remind them that they do not have to understand every word, but that they should look for key words to help them.
- Students can compare answers in pairs.
- Check the answers with the class, encouraging students to give evidence from the text for their answers where possible.

ANSWERS

a paragraph 3   b paragraph 2   c paragraph 1
d paragraph 4

Exercise 2

- Students read the text again and answer the questions.
- Remind them that they do not have to understand every word, but that they should use the key words in the questions to help them find the information they need.
- Students can compare answers in pairs.
- Check the answers with the class.

ANSWERS

1 He thinks they don't have a very healthy diet.
2 His favorite family meal is roast chicken, roast potatoes, vegetables and chocolate mousse for dessert.
3 In his free time he plays soccer, goes to the gym, listens to music, and watches TV.
4 When he leaves college he wants to be a food writer and own a restaurant.

Extra activity

- Give students a few minutes to read and memorize as much detail as they can from the text.
- Books closed. Ask students questions and see how much they can remember about Sam Stern, e.g. *How old is he? How many books has he written? What does he want teenagers to do?*

Consolidation

- Encourage students to make a note of any new words and expressions in their vocabulary books.

Listening

Aim

To listen to and understand a conversation between two teenagers talking about food

Warm-up

- Ask students to think about what food they think is in a healthy diet, and what food is in an unhealthy diet. Elicit responses and write them on the board.

Exercise 3 1.49

- Explain that students will hear two teenagers talking about the food they eat. They must write down all the food they hear, and then choose the correct option to describe the teenagers' diets.
- Play the CD. Students listen and write down the food.
- Students can compare answers in pairs.
- Check the answers with the class.
- Students then choose the correct option to describe Matt and Molly's diets.

ANSWERS / AUDIO CD TRACK 1.49

1 **Matt**   Hi! My name's Matt. This is what I eat in a typical day. I don't usually have breakfast because I don't have time in the morning, but I always eat a bar of chocolate on the way to school. Our morning break at school is at ten thirty. There's a snack machine at school and I usually buy a soda. I have a hot lunch at school and I always choose pizza or chicken and fries. When I get home, I have a snack in front of the TV. I usually have some cookies in the afternoon, too. Mom cooks dinner for the family at six o'clock. She wants us to eat healthy food, but my favorite dinner is a hamburger and fries. I sometimes have a banana, but I don't like fruit very much.

2 **Molly**   Hello. I'm Molly. Here's what I eat in a typical day. I don't have much time for breakfast, but I usually have a glass of milk and some cereal. We have a break at school at eleven o'clock and I always have some orange juice and a ham sandwich. I usually have lunch at school and I eat some chicken or fish and a salad. When I get home from school I help Mom cook. We eat at six thirty, when Dad gets home from work. My favorite dinner is pasta with tomatoes and then fruit salad for dessert.

1a Matt: chocolate, soda, pizza, chicken, fries, cookies, hamburger, banana
1b unhealthy
2a Molly: milk, cereal, orange juice, ham sandwich, chicken, fish, salad, pasta, tomatoes, fruit salad
2b healthy

Extra activity

- Ask students if any of the food they mentioned in the *Warm-up* was in Matt's or Molly's diet.

Speaking

Aim

To ask and answer questions about diet

Warm-up

- Ask students: *What have you eaten so far today? Do you think this is healthy or unhealthy?* You can tell them what you have eaten today too, to contribute to the conversation.

Exercise 4 Pairwork

- Give students time to read the survey questions. Check any vocabulary if necessary.
- In pairs, students ask and answer the questions.
- Monitor and check that students are taking turns to ask and answer questions and that their partner is making a note of their answers.
- Encourage them to work out the scores for each other when they have asked all the questions.

ANSWERS
Students' own answers.

Exercise 5

- Students report back to the class on their partner's diet using the information and the scores from exercise 4.
- Encourage students to suggest ways in which their partner can improve their diet.
- Students can vote on the person they think has the healthiest diet in the class.

ANSWERS
Students' own answers.

Extra activity 1

- Students can keep a food diary for the coming week. They can bring it back into class and discuss it.

Extra activity 2

- Students write out their ideal meal. They give their meal to their partner who gives it a score, based on the survey scores in exercise 4, for being healthy or unhealthy.

Writing

Aim

To write a short text about diet

Warm-up

- Write some food and drinks on the board and ask students to say if it is healthy or unhealthy, e.g. *cola, milk, water, carrots, cookies, apples*, etc.

Exercise 6

- Students read the questions before they begin writing.
- Remind them to make notes first and then to use their notes to produce a first draft.
- Students can swap drafts with a partner who corrects it.
- Students then write a final draft in class or for homework.

ANSWERS
Students' own answers.

Extra activity 1

- If students have completed their final draft for homework, ask them to bring their texts into the class and to tell other students about their diets.
- You can display the texts around the classroom.

Extra activity 2

- Students research a famous sportsperson they admire and find out what they eat. They can write about this for homework and decorate it with photos and illustrations.

CD-ROM **WORKBOOK PAGE W37**

Review

Grammar
Present progressive for future (Affirmative, negative, interrogative, short answers)
How long …? + take
Countable and uncountable nouns
a / an / some / any
How much …? / How many …?
a little / a few / much / many

Vocabulary
Transportation
Food and drink

Review C PAGES 68–69

Vocabulary

Exercise 1

ANSWERS

2 helicopter 3 bus 4 taxi 5 train 6 bike
7 motorcycle 8 boat 9 ferry

Exercise 2

ANSWERS

Across: orange, rice, tuna, bread, water
Down: chicken, milk, cheese, egg, juice

Grammar

Exercise 3

ANSWERS

Students' own answers.

Background notes

• The Pussycat Dolls are an American girl pop and dance group which was founded in 1995. Some of their hits include *Don't Cha* and *Stickwitu*.

Exercise 4

ANSWERS

1 How many concerts are they playing in Mexico?
They're playing one concert in Mexico.
2 When are the Pussycat Dolls playing in São Paulo?
They're playing in São Paulo on October 12th.
3 Where are they going after São Paulo?
They're going to Montevideo, Uruguay.
4 How many cities are they visiting in Latin America?
They're visiting six cities in Latin America.
5 How many concerts are they doing in Latin America?
They're doing six concerts in Latin America.
6 Where are the Pussycat Dolls finishing their tour?
They're finishing their tour in Buenos Aires, Argentina.

Exercise 5

ANSWERS

1 She is having pizza with her friends tomorrow night. ; 4
2 She is playing a volleyball game tomorrow afternoon. ; 3
3 She is going to Tracy's birthday party on the weekend. ; 5
4 She is staying with her aunt in Phoenix next week. ; 6
5 She is studying with Jane and Ann this evening. ; 2

Exercise 6

ANSWERS

1 How long does it take you to do your homework?
2 How long does it take you to get to your grandparents' house?
3 How long does it take you to read a book with 300 pages?
4 How long does it take you to take a shower?
5 How long does it take you to have your dinner?
Students' own answers.

Exercise 7

ANSWERS

Countable: 1 cookie **2** egg **3** sandwich
Uncountable: 4 bread **5** milk **6** water

Exercise 8

ANSWERS

1 any 2 an 3 an; a 4 any 5 some 6 any; some; some

Exercise 9

ANSWERS

1 How much 2 How many 3 How many 4 How much
5 How much 6 How many

Exercise 10

ANSWERS

1 much 2 much 3 any 4 some

Got it?

Exercise 11

ANSWERS

1 are you 2 takes 3 starting 4 many 5 some 6 any
7 a lot of 8 many

Exercise 12

ANSWERS

1 They're having a surprise birthday party for Paul.
2 It takes five minutes by bus.
3 The party is starting at eight o'clock.
4 Alice has a lot of food.
5 No, she doesn't (have many CDs).

Songs

The following songs would be appropriate to use at this point:

• *Sailing* by Gavin Sutherland (transportation, present progressive)
• *Thank you for the music* by ABBA (present progressive)
• *Tom's diner* by Suzanne Vega (food, present progressive)

Culture club

Grammar
Simple present
there is / are
some / a lot of

Vocabulary
Food and drink
Music

Topics
Restaurants and food
Fast food and healthy diets

Culture club C PAGE 70

Aim

To read and understand a text about a restaurant chain

Warm-up

- Ask students to look at the photos. Ask: *Do you know this restaurant? Have you eaten in this restaurant? If so, where? If not, would you like to? What type of food can you eat there?*

Background notes

- Hard Rock Café is a chain of restaurants founded in London in 1971 by Peter Morton. In 1979, the cafés started covering their walls with rock 'n' roll items, which has now become one of the themes in the cafés.

Exercise 1

- Before students read and answer the questions, ask them to read the text quickly and to find the names of three singers (Elvis Presley, Madonna, Gwen Stefani) and two bands (the Beatles, Nirvana).
- Students read the text and answer the questions.
- Remind them that they do not need to understand every word in the text, but they should look for key words in the questions to help them find the information they need for the answers.
- Students can compare their answers in pairs.
- Check the answers with the class, encouraging students to give evidence from the text where possible.

ANSWERS
1 There are 135 in the world.
2 50 countries have Hard Rock Cafés.
3 You can eat fast food like burgers and fries and also healthy food like chicken, salmon, and salads.
4 You can hear rock music.
5 There are some of Elvis Presley's clothes and some personal possessions from the Beatles, Nirvana, Madonna, and Gwen Stefani.
6 They often buy T-shirts.
7 You can read the name of the city where the restaurant is.

Exercise 2 Focus on you

- Students make notes on the questions on page 70 to prepare a short text.
- If students need more support with this, you can brainstorm ideas as a class and write their ideas on the board.
- They write a draft of their text and swap with a partner who checks it for mistakes.
- They write a final version.

ANSWERS
Students' own answers.

Extra activity
• If students have access to a computer they can present their text to the class using PowerPoint.

Extra activity
• If students are interested in the topic, they can do more research for homework and find out about other restaurant chains around the world.
• They can write a short text and bring it back into class the next day.

My progress PAGE 71

- For items 1–6, students read the sentences and complete the lists with their examples.
- If students have less than 3 / 5 for individual statements, encourage them to review the grammar or vocabulary and to do more practice.
- For items 7–10, students circle the answer which reflects the progress they have made in Units 5 and 6.
- If they have chosen *I'm not sure* or *No*, encourage them to review these sections and to do more practice.

7 That's better!

Grammar
Comparative adjectives (Short, long, and irregular adjectives)
as ... as
less ... than

Vocabulary
Geography

Communication
Asking for tourist information

Skills
Reading: A magazine article about bizarre pets
Listening: A pet shop owner giving advice
Speaking: Talking about your favorite animals
Writing: A paragraph about a pet

Topics
Geography
Animals: Pets

Presentation PAGE 72

Aim

To present the new language in a motivating context

Story

Zoe is helping Sam with his geography so he can get a better report card in the next test. He doesn't answer all of Zoe's questions correctly, but Zoe is impressed with what he knows.

Warm-up

- Ask students to look at the photo and ask: *Who can you see?* (Sam and Zoe) *Where are they?* (in the school computer room) *What do you think they are doing?*

Exercise 1 Read and listen 1.50

- Give students time to read the answer choices before they listen.
- Play the CD. Students read and listen and choose the correct subject.
- Stronger students can read the dialogue, choose the answer and then listen and check.
- Check the answer with the class.
- Go through the dialogue again and the *Check it out!* box as a class. Make sure that students understand any new words or phrases.
- Play the CD again. Students listen and repeat chorally, then individually.

Transcript STUDENT BOOK PAGE 72

ANSWER
c geography

Exercise 2 Comprehension

- Students complete the sentences with the words in the box.
- Remind them to refer back to the dialogue if necessary.
- Check the answers with the class.

ANSWERS
1 Mississippi; Sacramento 2 The Rockies; the Appalachians
3 New York; Los Angeles 4 New York 5 Los Angeles

Consolidation
- Remind students to make a note of any new words or phrases from the dialogue in their vocabulary books.

Language focus PAGE 73

Aim

To practice the target language in a new context

Exercise 3 Dialogue focus

- Students write the sentences in the correct order.
- Remind them to look at the photos or to refer back to the dialogue in exercise 1 if necessary.
- Do not check the answers at this point.

Exercise 4 1.51

- Play the CD. Students listen and check their answers.
- Students listen again and repeat.

ANSWERS / AUDIO CD TRACK 1.51
1 Zoe The Mississippi is longer than the Sacramento River. True or false?
  Sam I don't know. False?
2 Zoe [1]The Appalachian Mountains are higher than the Rockies. True or false?
  Sam That's true.
3 Sam [2] Ask me about cities. They're more interesting than boring mountains.
  Zoe [3] OK. Is New York bigger or smaller than Los Angeles?
  Sam Easy! New York is bigger.
  Zoe Correct. [4] You're almost as smart as me!

Exercise 5 Focus on you

- Students use the information in the chart and the phrases in the box and write sentences comparing the U.S. and Japan.
- Monitor and check.
- Ask one or two students to read out their sentences.

ANSWERS
Students' own answers.

Exercise 6 Pairwork

- In pairs, students now use the information in the chart in exercise 5 and compare Brazil with the U.S.
- Ask one or two pairs to read out their sentences.

ANSWERS
Students' own answers.

Vocabulary PAGE 74

Geography

Aim

To present and practice geography vocabulary: *continent, country, desert, island, lake, mountain, ocean, river, sea, volcano*

Background notes

- Barbados is an island situated in the Atlantic Ocean. The capital city is Bridgetown.
- The Sahara is the world's largest hot desert. It covers most of northern Africa and it is almost as big as the U.S.
- Asia is the world's largest continent. It covers approximately 8.6% of the Earth's total surface and there are about 4 billion people who live in Asia.
- The Nile is one of the major rivers in Africa and is thought to be the longest river in the world.
- The Mediterranean Sea is almost completely surrounded by land. It has coasts in Europe, Africa, and Asia.
- Lake Superior is the largest of the five great lakes of North America.
- Vesuvius is a volcano in southern Italy, east of the city of Naples. It is famous for its eruption in AD79, when it destroyed the cities of Pompeii and Herculaneum.
- Mount Everest is the highest mountain in the world at 8,848 meters. It is part of the Himalaya mountain range in Asia and it is on the borders of Nepal, Tibet, and China.
- Canada is the country that occupies most of North America. The capital city is Ottawa and the main languages spoken are French and English.

Warm-up

- Ask students about places in their country using the target vocabulary, e.g. *Are there any mountains in your county? What are they called? Are there any volcanoes?*, etc.

Exercise 1

- Students match the geographical features in column A with the names in column B.
- Students can compare their answers in pairs. Do not give the answers at this point.

Exercise 2 🔊 1.52

- Play the CD. Students listen and check their answers to exercise 1.
- Students listen again and repeat chorally, then individually.

ANSWERS / AUDIO CD TRACK 1.52

1 i mountain   Mount Everest
2 d river   the Nile
3 f lake   Lake Superior
4 a island   Barbados
5 c continent   Asia
6 j country   Canada
7 b desert   the Sahara
8 h volcano   Mount Vesuvius
9 e sea   the Mediterranean
10 g ocean   the Atlantic

Extra activity

- If you have a world map, you can put it on the board and ask students to come and identify the places in exercise 1.

Exercise 3

- Students look at the map and use the words in the box to complete the description of Hawaii.
- Students can compare their answers in pairs.
- Check the answers with the class.

ANSWERS

1 islands   2 volcanoes   3 mountain   4 sea   5 lake
6 river

Background notes

- The Amazon River is the second largest river in the world and it flows through Brazil, Peru, Bolivia, and Ecuador.
- The Paraná River flows through Brazil, Paraguay, and Argentina.
- Cerro Aconcagua (6,962 meters) is in the Andes mountain range in Mendoza, Argentina. It is the highest mountain outside Asia.
- Ojos del Salado is a huge volcano in the Andes mountain range on the border with Argentina and Chile. It is the highest volcano in the world, at 6,891 meters.
- Lake Maracaibo is in Venezuela. It is the largest lake in South America.
- Lake Titicaca is on the border of Bolivia and Peru.
- Grande de Tierra del Fuego is an island near the southern point of South America.
- The Galápagos islands are a group of volcanic islands in the Pacific Ocean near the equator, off the west coast of South America.
- The Caribbean Sea is situated north east of Central American countries such as Panama, Costa Rica, and Mexico. It is one of the largest saltwater seas.
- São Paulo is the largest city in Brazil.
- Bogotá is the capital of Colombia and it is the third highest capital city in the world.

Exercise 4 Pairwork

- Students read and complete the factfile for South America.
- Encourage them to use the Internet or an encyclopaedia if they need more help.

ANSWERS
Students' own answers.

Consolidation

- Remind students to make a note of the new vocabulary from this lesson in their vocabulary books. They can add small illustrations or translations if it will help them remember it more easily.

CD-ROM WORKBOOK PAGE W40

Grammar PAGE 75

Comparative adjectives (Short adjectives)

Aim

To present and practice short comparative adjectives

Warm-up

- Ask students some comparative questions about geographical features from the previous lessons, e.g. *Is Mount Everest higher than Mauna Kea in Hawaii?* (Yes, it is) *Is Los Angeles bigger than New York?* (No, it isn't), etc.

Grammar chart

- Go through the grammar chart with the class. Explain that we use comparative adjectives to talk about the differences between two people or things. We always use *than* after the adjective and before the second place or thing.
- Ask students to look back at the dialogue on page 72 and find more examples of short comparative adjectives.
- Draw students' attention to the form of short comparative adjectives and the spelling changes.

Rules PAGE W38

Exercise 1

- Students write sentences using the comparative form of the adjectives in parentheses.
- Check the answers with the class. Encourage students to spell out any comparatives with spelling changes.

ANSWERS

1 The Nile is longer than the Yangtze River.
2 Mount Everest is higher than Mount K2.
3 The Pacific Ocean is deeper than the Atlantic Ocean.
4 Willis Tower is taller than the Empire State Building.
5 Hawaii is hotter than Alaska (in the winter).

Exercise 2

- Individually or in pairs, students write sentences comparing Luiza and Marcella with the adjectives in the box.
- Check the answers with the class and encourage students to spell out any comparatives with spelling changes.

ANSWERS

1 Marcella is happier than Luiza.
2 Marcella is prettier than Luiza.
3 Marcella is shorter than Luiza.
4 Luiza is older than Marcella.
5 Luiza is slimmer than Marcella.
6 Marcella is younger than Luiza.

Comparative adjectives (Long adjectives)

Aim

To present and practice long comparative adjectives

Warm-up

- Ask students some questions using long adjectives and elicit answers from students, e.g. *Do you think math is more boring than English? Do you think girls are quieter than boys?*, etc.

Grammar chart

- Go through the grammar chart with the class. Explain that we use *more + than* with long adjectives, e.g. *more important than*, but that there are some two-syllable adjectives which take *-er*, e.g. *cleverer*.
- Ask students to look back at the dialogue on page 72 and find more examples of long comparative adjectives.
- Remind them to check the rules on page W38.

Rules PAGE W38

Exercise 3

- Students write sentences with the comparative form of the adjectives. Remind them to check if the adjective is long or short.
- Check the answers with the class, making sure that students are using *than* and the adjectives correctly.

ANSWERS

1 Skateboarding is more exciting than skiing.
2 Trains are slower than airplanes.
3 Chimpanzees are more intelligent than dogs.
4 The library is quieter than the gym.
5 Cell phones are more expensive than MP3 players.
6 Angelina Jolie is more famous than Julianne Moore.
7 Cars are safer than motorcycles.
8 Cats are more independent than dogs.

Comparative adjectives (Irregular adjectives)

Aim

To present and practice irregular comparative adjectives

Grammar chart

- Go through the grammar chart with the class. Explain that students will have to learn these forms.
- Remind them to check the rules on page W38.

Rules PAGE W38

Exercise 4

- Students complete the sentences with the comparative form of the adjectives.
- Remind them to check if the adjective is short, long, or irregular.
- Check the answers with the class.

ANSWERS

1 worse   2 prettier   3 further   4 easier   5 hotter
6 more interesting   7 safer

Finished?

- Students make a list of two singers / TV hosts / actors they know or like. They then write sentences about them using the comparative form of the adjectives in the box.

ANSWERS

Students' own answers.

Consolidation

- Remind students to make a note of the grammar and the rules from this lesson in their grammar books.

CD-ROM WORKBOOK PAGES W40–W41

Communication PAGE 76

Asking for tourist information

Aim

To present and practice the language for asking for tourist information

Background notes

- The Empire State Building is a popular tourist attraction in New York City. It sits between Fifth Avenue and West 34th Street. It is the tallest building in New York City.
- 5th Avenue is a major shopping area in the borough of Manhattan, New York.
- 34th Street is a major intersection in the borough of Manhattan, New York.

Warm-up

- Ask students: *Did you go on vacation last summer? Where did you go? Did you have to ask for information when you got there? Who did you ask?* and elicit replies.

Exercise 1 1.53

- Give students time to read the questions and the dialogue before they listen.
- Play the CD. Students listen and complete the dialogue with the missing questions.
- Encourage them to look at the information before and after each gap to help them choose the correct question.
- Stronger students can read and complete the dialogue and then listen and check.
- Play the CD. Students listen and check their answers.

ANSWERS / AUDIO CD TRACK 1.53

Assistant	Good morning. Can I help you?
Paula	Yes, please. I want to visit the Empire State Building. ¹How much are the tickets?
Assistant	They're $20 for adults and $14 for children.
Paula	²What time does it open?
Assistant	It's open from 8 a.m. to 2 a.m. every day. There aren't as many people there at 1 p.m. as at 11 p.m.
Paula	³Where is it?
Assistant	It's on 5th Avenue. Between 33rd and 34th Streets.
Paula	⁴How can I get there?
Assistant	You can take the subway to 34th Street or get a bus. The bus is as fast as the subway and you can see the city. Or you can walk. It takes about 45 minutes and it's less expensive than the bus or the subway!
Paula	Thanks.
Assistant	You're welcome. Have a nice day!

- Go through the *You ask, You answer* box with the class. Ask students to look back at the dialogue and find examples of the expressions in the box.

Exercise 2 Pronunciation 1.54

- Play the CD. Students listen and repeat chorally, then individually.
- Draw students' attention to the pronunciation of the schwa sound /ə/.

Transcript STUDENT BOOK PAGE 76

Exercise 3 1.55

- Play the CD. Students listen and circle the schwa sound in each word.
- Students listen again and repeat chorally, then individually.

ANSWERS / AUDIO CD TRACK 1.55

1 ex<u>e</u>rcise   2 op<u>e</u>n   3 childr<u>e</u>n   4 welc<u>o</u>me   5 Sat<u>u</u>rday
6 elev<u>e</u>n

Background note

- The Guggenheim Museum is in New York. It contains examples of impressionist, early modern, and contemporary art.

Exercise 4 1.56

- Give students time to read the factfile before they listen.
- Remind them to think about the sort of information they will be listening for, e.g. prices, times, and numbers.
- Play the CD. Students listen and complete the factfile.
- Students can compare answers in pairs.
- Students listen again and check their answers.

ANSWERS / AUDIO CD TRACK 1.56

Assistant	Good morning. Can I help you?
Man	Yes, please. I want to visit the Guggenheim Museum. How much are the tickets?
Assistant	They're $18 for adults, but children are free.
Man	OK, great. What time does it open?
Assistant	It opens at ten o'clock.
Man	And what time does it close?
Assistant	It closes at five forty-five.
Man	OK, fine. How can I get there?
Assistant	You can take the subway to 86th Street or take a bus.
Man	Thanks.
Assistant	You're welcome. Have a nice day!

1 $18   2 Free   3 10 a.m.   4 5.45 p.m.   5 subway or bus

Backgound note

- Madame Tussauds is a waxwork museum on West 42nd Street, New York.

Exercise 5 Pairwork

- In pairs, students use the information in the factfile to write a new dialogue about Madame Tussauds. Remind them to look back at the dialogue in exercise 1 if they need help.
- Students can act out their dialogues for the rest of the class.

ANSWERS

Students' own answers.

> ## Consolidation
> - Remind students to make a note of any new words or phrases from this lesson in their vocabulary books. Encourage them to write translations or use examples from their own country if it will help.

CD-ROM WORKBOOK PAGE W42

Grammar PAGE 77

as … as

Aim

To present and practice *as … as* with adjectives for comparisons

Warm-up

- Ask students one or two questions using *as … as* and elicit responses, e.g. *Is (Laura) as tall as (Paco)?*

Grammar chart

- Go through the grammar chart with the class. Elicit or explain that we use *as … as* to say how two things or people are the same, and *not as … as* to say how they are different. Elicit or explain that *as* goes before the adjective in each case.
- Ask students to look back at the dialogue on page 72 and find an example of *as … as*.
- Remind students to check the rules on page W39.

Rules PAGE W39

Exercise 1

- Students write sentences with *as … as* and the adjectives in the box.
- Remind students to think about the position of the adjective.
- Check the answers with the class.

ANSWERS
1 Dhaka is as big as Hong Kong.
2 Giraffes aren't as heavy as elephants.
3 Moscow is as cold as Chicago.
4 Koji's test wasn't as good as Emi's.
5 Mili is as tall as Lucas.
6 A burger isn't as expensive as a pizza.

Exercise 2

- Students rewrite the sentences using *as … as*.
- Remind them to think about the position of the adjectives when they are rewriting, and whether the adjective is regular or irregular.
- Students can compare answers in pairs.
- Check the answers with the class.

ANSWERS
1 Talent shows aren't as bad as reality shows.
2 Jim Carrey isn't as funny as Will Smith.
3 Math isn't as interesting as history.
4 The climate in Chile isn't as hot as the climate in Hawaii.
5 Taking the subway isn't as cheap as taking the bus.
6 Dogs aren't as clean as cats.

Extra activity

- In pairs, students think of two books, movies, or TV shows they like and choose two adjectives from exercise 2.
- Their partner must compare the two things using *as … as* and the adjective.

---

less … than

Aim

To present and practice *less … than* with adjectives for comparison

Grammar chart

- Go through the grammar chart with the class. Elicit or explain that *less … than* means the same as *not as … as*. Draw students' attention to the position of the adjective after *less*.
- Remind them to check the rules on page W39.

Rules PAGE W39

Exercise 3

- Students write sentences with *less … than* and give their opinion using the adjectives in parentheses.
- Remind students to think about the adjective and its position.
- Check the answers with the class.

ANSWERS
1 Trains are less expensive than buses.
  Buses are less expensive than trains.
2 MP3 players are less useful than cell phones.
  Cell phones are less useful than MP3 players.
3 Jay-Z is less famous than Daddy Yankee.
  Daddy Yankee is less famous than Jay-Z.
4 Action movies are less exciting than horror movies.
  Horror movies are less exciting than action movies.
5 Kirsten Stewart is less beautiful than Emma Watson.
  Emma Watson is less beautiful than Kirsten Stewart.
6 New York is less populated than Sydney.
  Sydney is less populated than New York.

Exercise 4 Game!

- In pairs, students think of two words for each category. They then ask their partner to say a comparative sentence about the two things.
- If their partner makes a correct sentence, they get one point. The student with most points is the winner.

ANSWERS
Students' own answers.

Finished?

- Students write their opinions about the places and things in exercise 4.
- They can swap sentences with a partner who corrects them.

ANSWERS
Students' own answers.

Consolidation

- Remind students to make a note of the grammar rules from this lesson in their grammar books. Encourage them to write examples comparing two different things.

CD-ROM WORKBOOK PAGE W41

Skills PAGES 78–79

Reading

Aim

To read and understand a magazine article about bizarre pets

Background notes

- Mexico is bordered to the north by the U.S., the Pacific Ocean on the south and west, and the Gulf of Mexico on the east. The capital is Mexico City.
- Italy is a country in central Europe. The capital city is Rome.
- Taranto is a city on the coast of southern Italy in the Puglia region of the country. It has a population of about 200,000.

Warm-up

- Ask students questions about pets, e.g. *Do you have any pets? If so, what animals do you have? If not, which animal would you like as a pet? Do you know anyone with an unusual pet? What is it?*

Exercise 1

- Before students read the text, ask them to look at the photos and the title and to predict what they think the text will be about.
- Ask them to read the text quickly to see if their predictions were correct. Explain that looking at a title and photos can help you understand what a text will be about before you read it.
- Students read the text again and answer the questions.
- Remind students to think about the information in the questions and what sort of information they need to look for in the text.
- Students can compare answers in pairs.
- Check the answers with the class.

ANSWERS

1 They are active at night.
2 They eat mice.
3 They are cheaper than other snakes.
4 It comes from the town of Taranto in Italy.
5 They eat insects.
6 Because they are poisonous and they bite.
7 It is less serious than people think.

> **Extra activity**
> - In pairs, students choose one of the pets and explain to their partner why they would like to have it.

Listening

Aim

To listen to a pet shop owner advising a boy about guinea pigs and hamsters

Warm-up

- Ask students to look at the photos. Ask them one or two questions, e.g. *Do you know the names of these animals? Do you know anyone who has one of these as a pet? Which one do you prefer?*

Exercise 2 1.57

- Give students a few minutes to read through the questions before they listen, and to think about the kind of information they will be listening for.
- Play the CD. Students listen and decide if the sentences are true or false.
- Students can compare answers in pairs.
- Check the answers with the class.

ANSWERS / AUDIO CD TRACK 1.57

Boy I want to buy a pet, but I can't decide between a guinea pig and a hamster. What are the differences?

Salesclerk Well, they're both rodents. They're part of the same family as rabbits and rats.

Boy Where are they from?

Salesclerk [1]Guinea pigs come from South America and hamsters come from Central Europe and Asia.

Boy Which are bigger?

Salesclerk Oh, [2]guinea pigs are definitely bigger than hamsters. They're usually about twenty centimeters long. [3]Hamsters are only about ten centimeters long.

Boy Do they live a long time?

Salesclerk Well, [4]guinea pigs usually live for four to five years and hamsters only live two or three years.

Boy Oh, no. That isn't good! But are they friendly?

Salesclerk Guinea pigs are friendlier than hamsters. [5]It's better to keep two or three guinea pigs together. Hamsters aren't as sociable. They don't like to live together.

Boy And do they bite?

Salesclerk [6]Hamsters sometimes bite. [7]They're more aggressive than guinea pigs.

Boy OK. [8]So, which are cheaper?

Salesclerk [9]Hamsters. A guinea pig costs twenty-five dollars. A hamster only costs ten dollars.

Boy OK. Mom, what do you think I should go for?

1 False 2 False 3 True 4 False 5 True 6 True
7 True 8 False

Exercise 3 1.57

- Play the CD again. Students listen and correct the false sentences from exercise 2.
- Students can compare answers in pairs.
- Check the answers with the class.

ANSWERS

1 Guinea pigs are from South America.
2 Guinea pigs are bigger than hamsters. (Guinea pigs are about 20 cm, hamsters are 10 cm.)
4 They usually live for four to five years.
8 Guinea pigs are more expensive than hamsters. (Guinea pigs cost $25, hamsters cost $10.)

> **Extra activity**
> - In pairs or small groups, ask students to discuss which pet they think the boy will choose.

Speaking

Aim

To talk about favorite animals and compare them

Warm-up

• Write the names of two animals on the board and brainstorm adjectives to describe them. Ask students which of the animals on the board they prefer and why.

Exercise 4 Pairwork

• In pairs, students choose a favorite animal from box A and tell their partner about it using the adjectives in box B.

• If students need help, go through the model dialogue with them and show them how to add extra information.

• Monitor and check that students are taking turns to ask and answer questions and to give their opinions. Make sure they are using comparatives correctly and make a note of any repeated errors to go over at the end of the lesson.

• Ask one or two pairs to report back to the class on their favorite animals.

ANSWERS

Students' own answers.

Extra activity

• For homework, students can design a poster featuring their favorite animal and explaining why it is a good pet.

• You can display the posters around the classroom.

Writing

Aim

To write a short paragraph about a pet you want to buy

Warm-up

• Ask students to look back at the reading text on page 78 and to give you the advantages and disadvantages for each pet.

• This can be done as a competition, with one half of the class looking at the corn snake and the other looking at the tarantula. The first half to list all the advantages and disadvantages correctly, is the winner.

Exercise 5

• In pairs or small groups, students choose a traditional and an exotic pet.

• They make notes on each question and prepare a first draft of their paragraph.

• Students can swap drafts with a partner who corrects the errors.

• If students need help with this exercise, you can brainstorm the names of pets and write them on the board. Then go through each question as a class and make a note of students' ideas on the board.

• Students then write a final draft. Remind them to use adjectives and comparative forms in their final versions.

ANSWERS

Students' own answers.

Extra activity 1

• Students can finish the writing exercise for homework and they can add illustration or photos.

• Encourage them to read out their finished paragraphs to the rest of the class.

Extra activity 2

• Students can research another traditional or exotic pet for homework and can write a short paragraph or design a poster about it.

CD-ROM WORKBOOK PAGE 43

8 The best day of my life!

Grammar
Superlative adjectives (Short, long, and irregular)
Comparative / Superlative
the least

Vocabulary
Feelings and emotions

Communication
Making a phone call

Skills
Reading: A magazine article about the effect of color on our emotions

Listening: Two teenagers talking about colors

Speaking: Asking and answering questions about favorite colors

Writing: A short text about favorite colors

Topics
Society: Emotional well-being
Multiculturalism: Colors and symbolism in different cultures

Presentation PAGE 80

Aim
To present the new language in a motivating context

Story
Teo and Zoe are talking to Sam about his report card, but he hasn't opened it yet. Sam goes home and his mom opens his report card to discover he has got his best results ever in the exams. She is delighted and he phones Coach Carson who says he can play in the basketball final on Saturday.

Warm-up
- Ask students to look at the photo. Ask: *Who can you see?* (Teo, Zoe, and Sam) *What do you think they are talking about?* (Sam's report card) *How do you think he is feeling?* (nervous).

Exercise 1 Read and listen 1.58
- Give students time to read the options before they listen.
- Play the CD. Students read and listen and choose the correct answer.
- Check the answer with the class.
- Go through the *Check it out!* box and the dialogue with the class.
- Play the CD again. Students listen and repeat chorally, then individually.

Transcript STUDENT BOOK PAGE 80

ANSWER
a very good

Exercise 2 Comprehension
- Students read the dialogue again and answer the questions.
- Students can compare answers in pairs.
- Check the answers with the class.

ANSWERS
1 The math exam was the worst.
2 The geography exam was the easiest.
3 The basketball final is on Saturday.

Consolidation
- Remind students to make a note of any new words or phrases from the dialogue in their vocabulary books.

Language focus PAGE 81

Aim
To practice the target language in a new context

Exercise 3 Dialogue focus
- Students read and complete the dialogues with the phrases in the box.
- Students can compare answers in pairs. Do not check the answers at this point.

Exercise 4 1.59
- Play the CD. Students listen and check their answers.
- Students listen again and repeat chorally, then individually.

ANSWERS / AUDIO CD TRACK 1.59
1 **Teo** Which exam was the worst?
   Sam Math was definitely [1]the most difficult. I was really nervous. But, thanks to Zoe, geography was [2]the easiest.
2 **Mom** Oh, Sam!
   Sam What?
   Mom These are [3]your best results ever!
   Sam Seriously?
3 **CC** Way to go, Sam! The final is on Saturday! Are you ready to play?
   Sam You bet! This is [4]the best day of my life!

Exercise 5 Focus on you
- Students write dialogues asking for and giving opinions about the things in the box.
- Monitor and check that they are using appropriate language for asking for and giving opinions, and make a note of any repeated errors to go over at the end of the lesson.

ANSWERS
Students' own answers.

Exercise 6 Pairwork
- In pairs, students practice the dialogues they wrote in exercise 5.

ANSWERS
Students' own answers.

Vocabulary PAGE 82

Feelings and emotions

Aim

To present and practice the vocabulary for feelings and emotions: *angry, annoyed, bored, confident, embarrassed, excited, fed up, frightened, happy, nervous, proud, sad*

Warm-up

- Draw one or two simple faces on the board with different expressions and elicit or give some adjectives for emotions, e.g. *happy, sad, angry*, etc.

Exercise 1 1.60

- Play the CD. Students read and listen to the adjectives.
- Students listen again and repeat chorally, then individually.

AUDIO CD TRACK 1.60

1 happy   2 nervous   3 proud   4 sad   5 frightened
6 bored   7 embarrassed   8 excited   9 confident
10 angry   11 annoyed   12 fed up

Exercise 2

- In pairs or individually, students classify the adjectives from exercise 1.
- Check the answers with the class.

ANSWERS

Positive: proud, excited, confident
Negative: sad, frightened, bored, embarrassed, angry, annoyed, fed up

Extra activity 1

- Give students a few minutes to look at and memorize as many adjectives as they can from exercise 1.
- Books closed. Draw one of the pictures from exercise 1 on the board. Students give you the adjective.

Extra activity 2

- In pairs, small groups or as a whole class, students act out an adjective from exercise 1 for the others to guess what it is.

Exercise 3

- Students read the sentences and choose the correct adjective.
- Remind them to think carefully about the meaning in each sentence.
- Students can compare answers in pairs.
- Check the answers with the class.

ANSWERS

1 angry   2 proud   3 embarrassed   4 sad   5 fed up

Extra activity

- Stronger students can write five sentences of their own with two adjective choices. They swap with a partner to choose the correct adjective.

Exercise 4 Pairwork

- In pairs, students ask and answer questions about their emotions using the ideas in the box.
- Monitor and check that students are asking and answering questions appropriately and make a note of any repeated errors to go over with the class at the end of the lesson.

ANSWERS
Students' own answers.

Extra activity

- Students ask and answer questions about how they would feel in the following situations, e.g. you get a bad grade in an exam, your team wins the final match in a competition, you hear a strange noise at night.

Consolidation

- Remind students to make a note of the adjectives from this lesson in their vocabulary books. Encourage them to add illustrations, translations, or their own examples to help them remember the adjectives.

CD-ROM   **WORKBOOK PAGE W46**

Grammar PAGE 83

Superlative adjectives (Short adjectives)

Aim

To present and practice short superlative adjectives

Warm-up

- Ask students how they are feeling today and elicit one or two adjectives, e.g. T: *Ana, how are you feeling today?* SS: *I'm feeling happy.*

Grammar chart

- Go through the grammar chart with the class. Elicit or explain that we use superlative adjectives to compare three or more things or people.
- Ask students to look back at the dialogue on page 80 to find examples of superlative adjectives.
- Go through the rules. You can explain that we often use *in* or *of* after a superlative adjective + noun, e.g. *the tallest student in the class, the best day of my life.*
- Remind them to check the rules on page W44.

Rules PAGE W44

Exercise 1

- Students write the superlative form of the adjectives. Remind them to check the grammar chart and the rules if necessary.
- Check the answers with the class. Ask students to spell out their answers to make sure they have made the spelling changes.

ANSWERS
1 the largest   2 the oldest   3 the hottest   4 the noisiest
5 the newest   6 the craziest   7 the closest   8 the reddest
9 the busiest

Exercise 2

- Students write sentences with the superlative form of the adjectives.
- Monitor and check that students are using the correct form of the adjective and direct them back to the rules if necessary.
- Students can compare their answers in pairs.
- Check the answers with the class.

ANSWERS
1 The living room is the biggest room in the house.
2 Uncle Richard is the funniest person in my family.
3 Fall is the prettiest season of the year.
4 Mark is the tallest boy in the class.
5 Today is the happiest day of my life.

Extra activity
- In pairs, students talk about the things in exercise 2 in relation to their own lives, e.g. the biggest room in their house, the funniest person in their family, etc.

Superlative adjectives (Long adjectives)

Aim

To present and practice long superlative adjectives

Grammar chart

- Go through the grammar chart with the class. Draw students' attention to the position of *the most* with long adjectives. Elicit or explain that adjectives of two syllables follow the same rules as short adjectives, e.g. *clever, the cleverest*, but that some adjectives can follow both patterns.
- Ask students to look back at the dialogue on page 80 and find an example of the superlative form of a long adjective.
- Elicit or give one or two more examples of long adjectives, e.g. *clever, narrow*, etc.
- Remind students to check the rules on page W44.

Rules PAGE W44

Exercise 3

- Students complete the sentences with the superlative form of the adjectives.
- Check the answers with the class.

ANSWERS
1 the most beautiful   2 the most difficult   3 the most dangerous   4 the most exciting   5 the most famous
6 the most expensive

Extra activity
- In pairs or as a whole class, ask students if they agree with the sentences in exercise 3.

Exercise 4

- Students complete the sentences with the superlative forms of the adjectives in the box.
- Remind them to think about word order and spelling.
- Check the answers with the class.

ANSWERS
1 the most expensive   2 the heaviest
3 the most populated   4 the fastest   5 the coldest

Extra activity
- For homework, students can find out more amazing facts about places, animals, or things in the world and write superlative sentences.

Finished?

- Students write sentences about the other students in their class and the subjects they study, using the superlative form of the adjectives in the box.
- They can swap sentences with a partner who corrects them.

ANSWERS
Students' own answers.

Consolidation
- Remind students to make a note of the grammar rules and explanations in their grammar books.

CD-ROM   WORKBOOK PAGES W46–W47

Communication PAGE 84

Making a phone call

Aim

To present and practice the language for making a phone call

Warm-up

- Ask students: *How often do you call your friends? Do you call them on your cell phone? What kind of things do you talk about?*

Exercise 1 1.61

- Give students time to read through the dialogues and the questions before they listen.
- Play the CD. Students listen and answer the questions.
- Students can compare answers in pairs.
- Play the CD again. Students listen and check their answers.
- You can copy the answer box onto the board and ask students to come out and fill in the answers before they listen and check.
- Students listen again and repeat chorally, then individually.

Transcript STUDENT BOOK PAGE 84

ANSWERS

Phone call 1: Becky is making the phone call. She wants to speak with Meg. No, she isn't successful.
Phone call 2: Harry is making the phone call. He wants to speak with Rick. Yes, he is successful.

- Go through the *You ask, You answer* box with the class. Ask students to look back at the dialogues and find examples of the different expressions.
- In pairs, students practice using the questions and answers in the box.

Extra activity

- In pairs, students can act out the dialogues in exercise 1. Stronger students can use their own names and choose different answers.

Exercise 2 Pronunciation 1.62

- Read the sentences out for students to hear the /h/ sound in each.
- Play the CD. Students listen and repeat chorally, then individually.

Transcript STUDENT BOOK PAGE 84

Exercise 3 1.63

- Give students time to read the words before they listen.
- Play the CD. Students listen and check the words they hear.
- Stronger students can check the words they think they will hear and then listen and check their predictions.
- Students listen again and repeat chorally, then individually.

ANSWERS / AUDIO CD TRACK 1.63

1 hand **2** his **3** at **4** I **5** hate

Extra activity

- If students need more practice with this sound, give them some more pairs of words, e.g. *him, in; here, ear; hi, eye*, etc.
- Students call out "h" if they hear the /h/ sound or remain silent if they don't.

Exercise 4 Pairwork

- In pairs, students read the instructions and prepare a short dialogue.
- If students need more help, encourage them to match each instruction with the lines of the dialogue in exercise 1.
- Monitor and check that students are taking turns to answer the phone.
- Students can act out their dialogues for the rest of the class.

ANSWERS

Students' own answers.

Extra activity

- Students can prepare a different phone dialogue and act it out with a new partner.

Consolidation

- Remind students to copy down any new words and phrases from this lesson in their vocabulary books. Encourage them to write translations if it will help them.

CD-ROM WORKBOOK PAGE W48

Grammar PAGE 85

Superlative adjectives (Irregular adjectives)

Aim

To present and practice irregular superlative adjectives

Warm-up

- Elicit or give the irregular adjectives students saw in Unit 7 (*good, bad, far*) and elicit the comparative forms (*better, worse, further*).

Grammar chart

- Go through the grammar chart with the class.
- Ask students to look back at the dialogue on page 80 and find an example of an irregular superlative.
- Remind students to check the rules on page W45.

Rules PAGE W45

Exercise 1

- Students complete the sentences with the superlative form of the adjectives in parentheses.
- Remind students that they must use *the* before a superlative.
- Check the answers with the class.

ANSWERS

1 the worst   2 the busiest   3 the furthest
4 the most interesting   5 the best

Comparative / Superlative

Aim

To present and practice the difference between comparative and superlative adjectives

Think! box

- Students read the *Think!* box and choose the correct option.
- Check the answers with the class.
- Remind students to check the rules on page W45.

ANSWERS

1 comparative   2 superlative

Rules PAGE W45

Exercise 2

- Students write sentences using the comparative and superlative form of the adjectives in parentheses.
- Remind students to think about word order and spelling.
- Check the answers with the class.

ANSWERS

1 Venezuela is bigger than Ecuador. Peru is the biggest.
2 A Volkswagen is more expensive than a Fiat. A Ferrari is the most expensive.
3 Aconcagua is higher than Mont Blanc. Mount Everest is the highest.
4 Caroline is taller than Joshua. Tom is the tallest.
5 Boston is hotter than London. Athens is the hottest.

Extra activity

- Students can write more examples like those in exercise 2. They can swap with a partner who writes sentences using comparative and superlative forms.

---

the least

Aim

To present and practice *the least*

Grammar chart

- Go through the grammar chart with the class. Elicit or explain that we use *the least* when we say something is less than the others. It is the superlative form of *less*.
- Draw students' attention to the position of *the least* before the adjective and explain that it can be followed by a noun, e.g. *the least interesting place*.
- Remind students to check the rules on page W45.

Rules PAGE W45

Exercise 3

- Students rewrite the sentences with *the least* and the adjectives in the box.
- Remind students to think about spelling and word order.
- Check the answers with the class.

ANSWERS

1 the least confident   2 the least interesting   3 the least difficult   4 the least noisy   5 the least dangerous

Exercise 4 Game!

- Students complete the sentences with the comparative or superlative form of the adjectives in parentheses.
- Students can compare answers in pairs.
- Students then decide if the answers are true or false.
- Check the answers with the class.

ANSWERS

1 São Paulo is <u>bigger than</u> New York. True
2 Uruguay is <u>the smallest</u> country in South America. False.
3 The Pacific Ocean is <u>the deepest</u> ocean in the world. True
4 Bill Gates is <u>the richest</u> man in the U.S. True
5 A Ferrari is <u>more expensive than</u> a Rolls-Royce. False
6 A giraffe <u>is faster than</u> an elephant. True

Finished?

- Students write three more questions for the quiz and ask their classmates if they are true or false.
- Students can use the Internet or an encyclopaedia to help them with their questions.

ANSWERS

Students' own answers.

CD-ROM WORKBOOK PAGES W46–W47

Skills PAGES 86–87

Reading

Aim

To read and understand a magazine article about colors and how they affect our emotions

Warm-up

• Ask students: *What is your favorite color? Why do you like it? Do you wear clothes in that color? How does the color make you feel?*

Exercise 1

• Before students read the text, ask them to look at the photos. Ask: *What is the woman in the first picture doing?* (she is getting married) *Who are the people in the second photo?* (doctors) *Which country do you think the people are from in the third photo?* (China).
• Students read the text quickly and match each heading to a paragraph.
• Remind students to look at the headings and find words in the text that will help them match the headings to the paragraphs.
• Check the answers with the class.

ANSWERS
1 Colors and our emotions   2 Relaxing colors
3 Positive, exciting colors   4 Cultural influences

Exercise 2

• Students read the text again and answer the questions.
• Remind them that they do not need to understand every word, but they should look for key information in the questions to help them find the answers.
• Students can compare answers in pairs.
• Check the answers with the class.

ANSWERS
1 Blue and green help us feel calm and relaxed.
2 They are positive because we feel happy and excited when we see them.
3 They can be negative because people can become impatient, irritable, and angry when they see them.
4 They wear white clothes to a funeral.
5 It symbolizes happiness and fortune.

Extra activity 1

• Give students a few minutes to read the text and memorize as much as they can.
• Books closed. In pairs or as a whole class, call out a color for students to give you the emotion associated with it.

Extra activity 2

• Read the first paragraph aloud sentence by sentence for students to copy out as a dictation exercise.
• Students can come out and write the sentences on the board.

Listening

Aim

To listen to and understand two teenagers talking about their favorite colors and how they affect their emotions

Warm-up

• Ask students: *What color is your bedroom? Did you choose the color? If so, why? If not, what color would you choose?*

Exercise 3 🔊 1.64

• Give students time to read the answer choices before they listen.
• Play the CD. Students listen and choose the correct answers.
• Students listen again and check.

ANSWERS / AUDIO CD TRACK 1.64

David My soccer team's colors are light blue and white, but I hate those colors. I think they're really boring. [1] I prefer stronger colors and I love red, blue, and black. At the moment, black is probably my favorite color and most of my clothes are black. I have a fantastic black and red jacket. It's really cool and [2] I always feel happy and confident when I wear it. I wanted black walls in my bedroom, but my parents said no. They suggested light green, but I hate that color. In the end, [3] I chose white because it's the opposite of black. I have white walls and black furniture. It looks cool!

Sonia A lot of my friends wear black clothes, but [4] I hate that color! I think it's sad and depressing. I prefer red, orange, and brown. [5] Orange is probably my favorite color. I have an orange winter coat and [6] I usually feel happy and more energetic when I wear it. It's old now, but I still like wearing it. I have a lot of orange in my bedroom, too. The duvet, curtains, and carpet are orange, but [7] the walls are light green. It's a good combination. The green helps me relax and study, and the orange keeps me happy!

1 likes   2 happy and confident   3 white   4 hates
5 orange   6 happy   7 light green

Extra activity

• Students design their ideal bedroom, thinking about the colors for the walls and furniture.
• They can draw the plans for their ideal bedroom for homework.

Speaking

Aim

To ask and answer questions about your favorite colors

Warm-up

- Ask students: *What are you wearing today? Why did you choose the color of your T-shirt / pants / sweatshirt?*, etc. *How do you feel when you wear that color?*

Exercise 4 Pairwork

- In pairs, students ask and answer the questions.
- Monitor and check that students are taking turns to ask and answer the questions. Make a note of any repeated errors to go over with the class at the end of the lesson.

ANSWERS
Students' own answers.

Exercise 5

- Ask pairs to tell the rest of the class about their partner's favorite colors and make a note of their answers on the board. Which colors were the most / least popular?
- Are there any interesting results? For example: *Do boys like different colors from girls? Is there a particular color that students in your class like? Why?*

ANSWERS
Students' own answers.

Extra activity

- In small groups, students can present the class's favorite colors as a wheel diagram or in a graph. They can use the information you noted on the board in exercise 5.

Writing

Aim

To write a short text about your favorite colors and how you feel about them

Warm-up

- Ask students: *Do you think colors really affect your emotions?* Encourage them to give examples.

Exercise 6

- Students make notes to answer the questions in exercise 4.
- They use their notes to write a first draft of their text.
- Students swap drafts with a partner who corrects their errors.
- Students then write a final draft.
- Students can add illustrations or decorations to their texts.

ANSWERS
Students' own answers.

Extra activity 1

- Students can do more research on other colors and how they affect your emotions for homework. They can write up the results as a text.

Extra activity 2

- Students can research a different culture and find out what different colors mean in that country. They can compare the information with their own culture and write a short report.

CD-ROM WORKBOOK PAGE W49

Grammar
Comparative and superlative adjectives (Long, short, and irregular)
as … as
less … than
the least

Vocabulary
Geography
Feelings and emotions

Review D PAGES 88–89

Vocabulary

Exercise 1

ANSWERS

2 country   3 ocean   4 island   5 volcano   6 lake
7 river   8 sea   9 mountain

Exercise 2

ANSWERS

1 frightened   2 angry   3 fed up   4 proud   5 happy
6 excited   7 nervous   8 embarrassed

Grammar

Exercise 3

ANSWERS

1 easier   2 warmer   3 better   4 nicer   5 more interesting
6 heavier   7 worse   8 safer   9 more talented   10 further

Exercise 4

ANSWERS

1 The computer isn't as expensive as the TV.
2 The computer isn't as big as the TV.
3 The computer isn't as heavy as the TV.
4 The computer isn't as popular as the TV.

Exercise 5

ANSWERS

1 … less famous than Justin Timberlake.
2 … less expensive than cars.
3 … less populated than Japan.
4 … less active than Mount St Helens.

Exercise 6

ANSWERS

1 the easiest   4 the nicest
2 the most important   5 the most popular
3 the best   6 the worst
Students' own answers.

Exercise 7

ANSWERS

Students' own answers.

Got it?

Exercise 8

ANSWERS

1 of the best   2 as popular as   3 more interesting
4 smaller   5 less   6 more active   7 more   8 the most

Exercise 9

ANSWERS

1 Florida is in the south-east of the U.S.
2 Turtle Beach is more interesting because there are a lot of animals and birds.
3 Manatees are smaller than elephants and they live in water.
4 Alligators are less dangerous than people think because they are frightened of humans and they are more active at night than in the day.
5 The most popular tourist attractions in the U.S. are Disney World and Universal Studios.

Songs

The following songs would be appropriate to use at this point:

- *Hold me* by Weezer (comparatives)
- *Sunshine on a rainy day* by Emma Bunton (feelings and emotions)
- *Boris the spider* by The Who (*as … as* and topic of spiders)

Culture club

Grammar
Comparatives and superlatives

Vocabulary
Measurement

Topics
World records

Culture club PAGE 90

Aim

To read and understand a text about world records

Warm-up

- Ask students to look at the photos. Ask: *Which world records do you think the photos represent?* Elicit ideas and ask students to read the text quickly to check their predictions.

Exercise 1

- Ask students to read the text quickly and find the answers to the following questions: *When did the Guinness Book of Records start?* (1951) *When did a pig jump 70 cm?* (August 2004) *Where was the tallest man in the world born?* (Illinois) *Where did the world's longest karaoke take place?* (Seoul) *How much beef was there at the world's biggest barbeque?* (12,000 kg).
- Students read the text and answer the questions.
- Remind them to look for key words in the questions to help them find the answers.
- Students can compare answers in pairs.
- Check the answers with the class.

ANSWERS
1 It is a famous book of world records about people, animals, and the natural world.
2 It is the best-selling non-religious book in the world.
3 He was 2.72 m tall.
4 She sang 1,200 songs.
5 It was in Uruguay.
6 It jumped 70 cm.

Extra activity
- In pairs, students choose a world record from the text. Give them a few minutes to read and memorize as much as they can. Their partner asks them questions to see how much they remember.

Exercise 2 Focus on you

- In class or for homework, students find out about a world record holder from their country and write a short paragraph.
- Remind them to make notes for each point and to write a first draft.
- They can swap drafts with a partner who corrects the mistakes.
- Students then write a final draft. They can include photos if they have found any.

ANSWERS
Students' own answers.

Extra activity
- If students are interested in the topic, the class can make their own Guinness Book of Records for their country. They can collect all the work students did in exercise 2 and put them together as a book.

My progress PAGE 91

- For items 1–6, students read the sentences and complete the lists with their examples.
- If students have less than 3 / 5 for individual statements, encourage them to review the grammar or vocabulary and to do more practice.
- For items 7–10, students circle the answer which reflects the progress they have made in Units 7 and 8.
- If they have chosen *I'm not sure* or *No*, encourage them to review these sections and to do more practice.

Grammar
Simple present
There is / There are
Adverbs of frequency

Vocabulary
Musical instruments and genres
Prepositions of place

Project
Write a magazine review about your favorite singer or band

Topic
Music: How different kinds of orchestras work
History: The origins of an orchestra

Curriculum extra A: Music PAGES C1–C2

Warm-up
- Ask students to look at the photo. Ask: *Do you play a musical instrument? If so, which one? If not, would you like to play an instrument? Have you ever listened to an orchestra? Does your school have an orchestra?*

Exercise 1
- In pairs, students read the text quickly and label the parts of the orchestra.
- Remind students that they do not need to understand every word in the text, but they should look for words that will help them to label the different parts.
- Check the answers with the class.
- You can copy the diagram onto the board and ask students to come out and label the diagram.

ANSWERS
1 percussion
2 brass
3 woodwind
4 strings
5 conductor

Exercise 2
- In pairs or individually, students read the text again in detail and correct the mistakes in each sentence.
- Remind them that they do not need to understand every word in the text, but encourage them to use the *Useful language* box and their dictionaries to help them.
- Check the answers with the class.

ANSWERS
1 Orchestras sometimes play <u>pop music</u> and <u>music for movies</u>.
2 There are about <u>fifty</u> musicians in a chamber orchestra.
3 There are <u>four</u> different groups of instruments in a symphony orchestra.
4 Violins and harps are in the <u>strings</u> section.
5 The conductor stands <u>in front of</u> the musicians.
6 The conductor knows the music for <u>all</u> the instruments.

Exercise 3
- Individually or in pairs, students answer the questions.
- Encourage them to think about the type of information they need to look for in the text, e.g. numbers, names of instruments, etc. Remind them to use dictionaries to help them.
- Check the answers with the class.

ANSWERS
1 The word *symphony* means "sound together".
2 There are four groups of instruments.
3 There are usually between sixty and seventy string instruments.
4 There are usually between two and five trumpets.
5 The conductor uses a baton to conduct.

Extra activity 1
- Write the word *symphony orchestra* on the board. Give students two minutes to see how many other words they can make from it.
- The student with the most correct words is the winner.

Extra activity 2
- Give students a few minutes to read the text again and to memorize as much detail as they can.
- In pairs or as a whole class, students test each other on what they can remember about an orchestra, e.g. *Which section are the violins in?* (string) *How many people are in a classical orchestra?* (about 100), etc.

Project
- In class or for homework, students write a magazine review about their favorite singer or band.
- Encourage them to make notes on each prompt first, and then to write a first draft.
- Students can swap drafts with a partner who corrects any mistakes.
- They can then produce a final draft and add photos or illustrations if they want.
- You can display the reviews around the class.

Consolidation
- Remind students to make a note of any new words or phrases from the lesson in their vocabulary books. Encourage them to add illustrations or translations if it will help them.

Grammar
Simple past (Regular and irregular verbs)

Vocabulary
Movies

Project
Write a review of your favorite movie

Topic
History: A history of movie production
Social science: Popular culture

Curriculum extra B: Media studies PAGES C3–C4

Background notes
- Eadweard Muybridge was an English photographer who was born in 1830 and died in 1904. He is best known for his work with cameras and capturing motion.
- The Lumière brothers were French and are thought to be amongst the earliest movie-makers in the world.
- Walt Disney, see Unit 4, page 48.
- *Snow White* was a 1937 Disney movie featuring the character Snow White, seven dwarfs, and a wicked stepmother. It was the first full-length cel-animated feature movie. It was the first full color movie Disney produced.
- Pixar Animation Studios is an American computer generated animation company. They are based in California. The company was bought by Disney in 2006.
- *Toy Story* was the first CGI feature movie from Pixar Studios in 1995.
- *King Kong* is a gigantic gorilla who featured in a 1933 movie and then again in a re-make in 2005.

Warm-up
- Ask students to look at the photos. Ask: *Do you recognize any of the characters? Have you seen the movies? Do you go to the movies? How often do you go? Who do you go with? Do you prefer to watch DVDs?*

Exercise 1
- Individually or in pairs, students read the text quickly and match the type of animation with the dates.
- Remind them that they do not need to understand every word in the text, but that they should look for the key words *(types of animation)* to help them find the answers.
- Check the answers with the class.
- You can copy the timeline onto the board and ask students to come out and complete it with the dates.

ANSWERS
1895: cinematograph
1928: animated cartoon
1937: cartoon movie
1960s: CGI
1995: first CGI movie

Exercise 2
- Individually or in pairs, students read the text again in detail and decide if the sentences are true or false. They correct the false sentences.
- Remind then that they do not need to understand every word in the text, but they can use the *Useful language* box to help them and their dictionaries.
- Check the answers with the class. Encourage students to give you evidence from the text for their answers.

ANSWERS
1 False. The zoopraxiscope produced the earliest form of animation.
2 True.
3 True.
4 True.
5 False. A complicated scene in *Toy Story* took up to thirty hours to make.

Exercise 3
- Individually or in pairs, students read the text and answer the questions.
- Encourage them to check any new words in a dictionary and to use the *Useful language* box to help them.
- Check the answers with the class.

ANSWERS
1 They used thin pieces of plastic called cels.
2 It was important because it was the first cartoon movie with sound.
3 It took three years to make *Snow White*.
4 *Toy Story* was special because it was the first computer-generated movie.
5 Twenty-seven animators worked on it.
6 The 2005 version used CGI to create the special effects.

Extra activity
- In pairs or small groups, students discuss what kind of movies they prefer and why.
- Ask pairs or groups to report back to the rest of the class.

Project
- In class or for homework, students write a review of their favorite movie.
- Encourage them to make notes on each prompt first, and then to write a first draft.
- Students can swap drafts with a partner who corrects any mistakes.
- They can then produce a final draft and add photos or illustrations if they want.
- You can display the reviews around the class.

Consolidation
- Remind students to make a note of any new words or phrases from the lesson in their vocabulary books. Encourage them to add illustrations or translations if it will help them.

Grammar
There is / There are
Simple past

Vocabulary
Transportation
Food

Project
Write a story about the journey of your food to your plate

Topic
Society: Helping people earn a better wage
Multiculturalism: Food around the world
Health and diet

Curriculum extra C: Citizenship `PAGES C5–C6`

Background notes
- The Caribbean is the region of the Caribbean Sea and its islands. There are more than 7,000 islands.
- El Guabo is a town in El Oro province in Ecuador. Banana farmers in El Guabo are using their co-operative model to help other farmers in Ecuador and throughout the world.

Warm-up
- Ask students to look at the photos. Ask: *Do you recognize the logo? What does it mean? Do you see food with this logo a lot in your country? Why is this logo important for farmers?*

Exercise 1
- Individually or in pairs, students read the text quickly and find out how many fair trade products it mentions.
- Remind them that they do not need to understand every word in the text. Encourage them to think about the information they need to look for to answer the question.
- Check the answer with the class. Encourage students to tell you what the products are.

ANSWER
5: chocolate, bananas, tea, coffee, soccer balls.

Exercise 2
- Students read the text again and match the titles to the paragraphs.
- Remind them to think about what each paragraph is telling them to help them find the right heading.
- Check the answers with the class.

ANSWERS
2 B
3 C
4 E
5 A

Exercise 3
- Individually or in pairs, students read the text and answer the questions.
- Remind them to think about the sort of information they will be looking for to find the answers. Encourage them to use the *Useful language* box or a dictionary to help with any new words and phrases.
- Check the answers with the class.

ANSWERS
1 Big international companies take the profits.
2 It is a business organization. It belongs to a group of people and they all work together for everyone.
3 They work in developing countries.
4 It helps them because they can earn more money from their crops and they can have a better future.
5 Bananas are one of the world's most popular fruits.

Exercise 4
- In pairs, students put the pictures in the correct order.
- Check the answers with the class.
- You can draw some simple pictures on the board and ask students to come out and write the correct numbers on them.

ANSWERS
A 4 B 3 C 6 D 1 E 5 F 2

Extra activity
- In small groups, students think of other fair trade products they know about. They can discuss how they think buying the products helps the farmers.

Project
- In class or for homework, students write about the journey their favorite food makes to reach their plates.
- Encourage them to make notes on each prompt first and then to write a first draft.
- Students can swap drafts with a partner who corrects any mistakes.
- They can then produce a final draft and add photos or illustrations if they want.
- You can display the stories around the class.

Consolidation
- Remind students to make a note of any new words or phrases from the lesson in their vocabulary books. Encourage them to add illustrations or translations if it will help them.

Grammar
Comparative and superlative adjectives

Vocabulary
Geography

Project
Write an article for a geography website about a volcano

Topic
Geography: Volcanoes

Curriculum extra D: Geography `PAGES C7–C8`

Background notes

- Mauna Loa is the largest volcano in the world. It is in Hawaii. Its name means "Long mountain". The volcano has been erupting for more than 700,000 years. The most recent eruption was in 1984.

Warm-up

- Ask students to look at the photos. Ask: *Do you know what this is? Is there a volcano in your country? Is it active or not?*

Exercise 1

- Individually or in pairs, students read the text quickly and answer the question.
- Remind them that they do not need to understand every word in the text. Encourage them to think about the information they need to answer to the question (a number).
- Check the answer with the class.

ANSWER
about 1,500

Exercise 2

- Students read the text again and label the diagram.
- Check the answers with the class.
- You can copy the diagram onto the board and ask students to come out and label it.

ANSWERS
2 lava
3 pipe
4 magma chamber

Exercise 3

- Individually or in pairs, students read the text in detail and answer the questions.
- Remind them to think about the sort of information they will be looking for to find the answers. Encourage them to use the *Useful language* box or a dictionary to help with any new words and phrases.
- Check the answers with the class.

ANSWERS
1 They are large, thin pieces of rock on the Earth's crust.
2 They are often near the places where the tectonic plates meet.
3 Because the Earth's plates are always moving.
4 Magma is the hot liquid inside the volcano; lava is the magma in an eruption.
5 The hot magma explodes through the holes in the Earth's crust.
6 It is a volcano in Hawaii. It is the largest volcano in the world.

Extra activity

- Give students a few minutes to read and memorize as much as they can about volcanoes.
- Books closed. In pairs or small groups, students have two minutes to write down as many words as they can that are connected with volcanoes.
- The pair or group with the most correct words is the winner.

Project

- In class or for homework, students write an article for a geography website about a volcano.
- Encourage them to make notes on each prompt first and then to write a first draft.
- Students can swap drafts with a partner who corrects any mistakes.
- They can then produce a final draft and add photos or illustrations if they want.
- You can display the articles around the class.

Consolidation

- Remind students to make a note of any new words or phrases from the lesson in their vocabulary books. Encourage them to add illustrations or translations if it will help them.

Workbook answer key

Unit 1

Vocabulary

Physical descriptions

Exercise 1
1 brown 2 heavy 3 tall 4 blond
5 freckles

Exercise 2
1 glasses 2 beard 3 hair 4 slim
5 curly 6 long

Exercise 3
Students' own answers.

Grammar

Simple present / Present progressive

Exercise 4
1 cooks
2 now
3 go
4 Do you always play
5 every day
6 isn't working

Exercise 5
1 Sue goes shopping three times a week.
2 Is Jack watching the movie at the moment?
3 Does Julie speak German?
4 They aren't studying at the moment.
5 The phone is ringing now.
6 Do you usually come to school by bus?
7 I'm not using the computer at the moment.
8 Does Tom play tennis on Mondays?

Exercise 6
1 A How often does Karen go swimming?
  B She likes swimming a lot!
2 A Are the boys using the Internet at the moment?
  B Yes, they are. They're writing an e-mail to Grandma.
3 A What do you do in the evenings?
  B I usually play computer games or I watch TV.
4 A What's Mom doing?
  B She's cooking dinner.

Possessive pronouns

Exercise 7
1 his 2 their 3 yours 4 hers
5 ours 6 yours

Exercise 8
1 mine 2 Their 3 Hers 4 yours
5 its 6 Ours

Adverbs of manner

Exercise 9
1 slowly 2 quickly 3 badly
4 early 5 happily 6 well

Exercise 10
1 quickly 2 slowly 3 early
4 badly 5 well 6 happily

Round-up

Exercise 11
1 at the moment
2 do you go
3 mine
4 well
5 your
6 once a week

Exercise 12
1 'm writing
2 speak
3 well
4 don't say
5 our
6 quickly
7 go
8 mine
9 are relaxing
10 is reading
11 are you doing

Communication

Making requests

Exercise 1
1 you can
2 Can I borrow
3 Not now
4 I'm doing
5 Can I have
6 you can't

Exercise 2
2 d 3 e 4 a 5 f 6 c

Exercise 3
1 Can I wear
2 No, you can't
3 Can't I use
4 Not now
5 You can use it later
6 Can I close
7 Yes, you can

Exercise 4
1 Can I read your journal?
  No, you can't.
2 Can I use your cell phone?
  Not now. I'm waiting for an important phone call.
3 Can I have a snack?
  Yes, you can.
4 Can I borrow your MP3 player?
  Not now. You can borrow it later.

Exercise 5
1 Can I sit down next to you?
  Yes, you can.
2 Can I use the DVD player (and watch a DVD)?
  No, you can't. Dinner is ready now. You can use it later.
3 Can I borrow your calculator? Mine is at home.
  Yes, you can. Here it is.

Skills

Reading

Exercise 1
1 She's South Korean.
2 She's on a study vacation.
3 It's pretty and historic. It has beautiful architecture.
4 She's staying with a host family.
5 He has blue eyes and blond, curly hair.
6 She goes five days a week from 9 a.m. to 1 p.m.
7 They come from South America, China, and Europe.
8 They use English.

Writing

Exercise 2
Students' own answers.

Unit 2

Vocabulary

Musical genres and instruments

Exercise 1
1 drums   2 trumpet   3 saxophone
4 guitar   5 recorder   6 piano
7 violin
Secret word: musical

Exercise 2
1 violinist   2 harpist   3 trumpeter

Grammar

be: Simple past (Affirmative)

Exercise 3
1 was   2 were   3 were   4 was
5 were   6 was

Exercise 4
1 Paul and Amy <u>were</u> at the movies.
2 The dog <u>was</u> in the garden.
3 The tickets <u>were</u> very expensive.
4 I <u>was</u> a student at Northwood School.
5 We <u>were</u> very tired.
6 You <u>were</u> late for your music lesson.

be: Simple past (Negative)

Exercise 5
1 wasn't   2 weren't   3 weren't
4 weren't   5 wasn't   6 wasn't
7 weren't   8 wasn't

Past time expressions

Exercise 6
1 afternoon   2 evening   3 Saturday
4 week   5 ten minutes   6 three days

Exercises 7 and 8
   Jack was at basketball training last
   night. 3
1 Jack and I weren't at Ian's party last
   Friday. 6
2 Jack and I were at school yesterday
   morning. 5
3 Jack was on vacation in Mexico last
   summer. 7
4 Jack wasn't in the library ten minutes
   ago. 1
5 Jack wasn't in his bedroom an hour
   ago. 2
6 Jack and Emma were at the gym
   yesterday afternoon. 4

be: Simple past (Interrogative and short answers)

Exercise 9
1 Was Ben at the pizzeria on Friday
   night? Yes, he was.
2 Was Luciano Pavarotti a famous blues
   singer?
   No, he wasn't. He was an opera singer.
3 Was the English test easy?
   No, it wasn't. It was difficult.
4 Was the documentary on the radio?
   No, it wasn't. It was on the TV.
5 Was Saturday December 1st?
   No, it wasn't. It was December 2nd.
6 Were Peter and Jim at school today?
   Yes, they were.

Question words + *was / were*

Exercise 10
1 Where were Oliver and his friends on
   Monday?
2 When was Oliver at his grandparents'
   house?
3 He was at soccer practice.
4 Where were Oliver and Patrick on
   Thursday? They were at chess club.
5 Who was Oliver with on Friday?
6 Why was Oliver at Tim's house on
   Saturday?

Round-up

Exercise 11
1 weren't   2 was   3 Was   4 was
5 were   6 was   7 Was   8 guitarist
9 wasn't   10 was   11 were   12 was

Communication

Agreeing and disagreeing

Exercise 1
1 I like 30 Seconds to Mars.
2 So do I. I think they're fantastic.
3 And I like Tokio Hotel, too.
4 Really? I don't.
5 Look, it's Katy Perry. I don't like her.
6 Neither do I.
7 And I don't like Daniela Mercury.
8 Really? I do. She's great.

Exercise 2
1 I don't   2 I don't   3 I do   4 I don't

Exercise 3
1 like
2 I don't
3 like
4 like
5 I don't
6 I like
7 I don't

Exercise 4
Students' own answers.

Skills

Reading

Exercise 1
1 Live Aid
2 ALAS
3 July 13th, 1985
4 May 17th, 2008
5 London, Philadelphia, Moscow, Sydney
6 Buenos Aires, Mexico City
7 about $63 million
8 more than $200 million

Exercise 2
1 The aim was to help people in Africa.
2 They were British.
3 U2, Queen, Elton John, Madonna, Bob
   Dylan.
4 The aim was to help poor children in
   Latin America.
5 Shakira, Ricky Martin, Alejandro Sanz.

Writing

Exercise 3
Students' own answers.

Unit 3

Vocabulary

Jobs

Exercise 1
1 factory worker   2 accountant
3 engineer   4 electrician   5 journalist
6 postal worker   7 hairdresser
8 teacher   9 lawyer   10 office worker

Exercise 2
1 accountant, office worker
2 For example: teacher, journalist
3 doctor, teacher
4 journalist, lawyer

Grammar

Simple past: Regular verbs (Affirmative)

Exercise 3
1 Jade washed her hair last night.
2 Mom talked to my math teacher yesterday.
3 I asked the teacher a question.
4 They opened a new library last summer.
5 He waited for the bus for half an hour.

Simple past: Regular verbs (Spelling variations)

Exercise 4
1 cried   2 lived   3 preferred   4 tried
5 studied
6 used   7 planned

Exercise 5
1 lived   2 arrived   3 tried   4 cried
5 visited   6 watched   7 played

Simple past: Irregular verbs

Exercise 6
Horizontal: drank, said, gave, bought
Vertical: thought, sent, wrote

Exercise 7
1 came   2 ran   3 gave   4 took
5 put   6 had; went   7 drank
8 read; wrote

Exercise 8
1 c Christopher Columbus discovered America.
2 b Brazil won the Football World Cup in 1958 and 1962.
3 b The first American president was George Washington.
4 c The first Olympic Games took place in Greece.
5 a In 1624 Dutch colonists bought Manhattan island from Native Indians for $24.

Exercise 9
1 do; did
2 'm listening; gave
3 bought; 's playing
4 eat; ate
5 sent; 'm writing
6 go; took

Round-up

Exercise 10
1 left   2 arrived   3 were   4 wanted
5 walked   6 looked   7 got   8 saw
9 watched   10 came   11 ate

Communication

Apologizing and making excuses

Exercise 1
1 I'm sorry, but I don't have my English book today.
2 I left it at home.
3 Oh, I'm sorry. It's at home.

Exercise 2
1 I left my jacket in the library
2 I have basketball practice
3 It doesn't matter
4 I'm using it at the moment
5 I can borrow Anthony's dictionary

Exercise 3
1 I'm sorry. I went to the movie theater.
2 I'm sorry. The bus was late.
3 I'm sorry. I don't have (any) credit at the moment.
4 I'm sorry. I'm writing an e-mail at the moment.
5 I'm sorry. The train was late.
6 I'm sorry. I don't have (any) money.

Exercise 4
1 A Excuse me. What's the time, please?
   B I'm sorry, I don't know. I don't have a watch.
2 A Let's go bowling this evening.
   B I'm sorry. I have a guitar lesson.
   A Don't worry. Why don't we go tomorrow evening?
   B OK. That's great.
3 A Why are you late?
   B I'm sorry. I took the wrong bus.
   A It doesn't matter. The movie starts at 8.30 and I have the tickets.
4 A Do you want to play a computer game with me?
   B I'm sorry. I'm watching TV at the moment.
   A What are you watching?
   B I'm watching a really good movie. It's nearly finished and I can play after the movie.

Skills

Reading

Exercise 1
2 False. It started in Mrs O'Leary's barn.
3 False. It didn't rain on the day the fire began.
4 False. There were 200 firefighters.
5 True.
6 False. It destroyed 17,000 buildings.
7 False. It burned for two days and one night.
8 False. People from all over the country sent money.

Writing

Exercise 2
Students' own answers.

Unit 4

Vocabulary

Movies

Exercise 1
1 comedy   2 thriller   3 animated
4 horror   5 fantasy   6 love
7 science fiction   8 action

1 animated movie
2 horror movie
3 fantasy movie
4 science fiction movie

Exercise 2
1 fantasy movie
2 animated movie
3 science fiction movie
4 love story
5 thriller

Grammar

Simple past (Negative)

Exercise 3
1 They didn't have a pizza.
2 Tom didn't go to the Chinese restaurant.
3 Anna and Leo didn't do their homework.
4 Jill didn't catch a bus.
5 Tom didn't buy a T-shirt.

Exercise 4
1 didn't play   2 didn't do   3 didn't go
4 didn't send   5 didn't watch

Exercise 5
Students' own answers.

Simple past (Interrogative and short answers)

Exercise 6
1 did   2 didn't   3 Did you buy
4 did   5 get   6 didn't

Exercise 7
1 Did you have a birthday party?
2 Did you take the bus to school today?
3 Did you take a shower this morning?
4 Did you see your cousins on the weekend?
5 Did you watch a movie on the weekend?
Students' own answers.

Question words + Simple past

Exercise 8
1 What time did the bus leave?
  It left at 8:15 a.m.
2 What did they do in the morning?
  They visited the White House.
3 Where did they have lunch?
  They had lunch in President's Park.
4 When did they visit the Museum of American History?
  They visited it in the afternoon.
5 What time did the bus arrive back at school?
  It arrived back at 6:00 p.m.

Round-up

Exercise 9
1 you do
2 we didn't
3 didn't see
4 Did you
5 took
6 Did you
7 went
8 we did

Communication

Buying a movie ticket

Exercise 1
2 B It's at 8 p.m.
3 A OK. Can I have one adult ticket and two children's tickets, please?
4 B Yes, sure. Where do you want to sit?
5 A In the center, please.
6 B OK, that's $25.
7 A Here you are.
8 B $30, thank you. Here are your tickets and $5 change.
9 A Which screen is it, please?
10 B It's screen 7.
11 A Thanks.

Exercise 2
1 B Yes, sure. That's $28.
2 A What time is the next screening of *Into the Wild*?
  B It's at 9:30.
3 A Which screen is *The Spiderwick Chronicles* on?
  B It's on screen 7.

Exercise 3
1 Clerk It's at 6:30 p.m.
2 You   OK. Can I have one adult ticket and three children's tickets, please?
3 Clerk Yes, sure. That's $26.
4 You   Here you are.
5 Clerk $40, thank you. Here are your tickets and $14 change.
6 You   Which screen is it on?
7 Clerk It's on screen 5.
8 You   Thanks. Bye.

Exercise 4
1 A Can we [1]have one adult ticket and one over 60s ticket for the 9 p.m. screening of [2]*Nim's Island*, please?
  B Yes, sure. That's [3]$17.
  A Here you are.
  B Thank you. *Nim's Island* is [4]on screen 1.
2 A Can I have two adult tickets and one children's ticket for *Happily N'Ever After*?
  B Yes, sure. That's $34.
  A Here you are.
  B $50, thank you. Here are your tickets and $16 change.

Skills

Reading

Exercise 1
1 He's almost 200 years old.
2 He speaks ten languages.
3 He first appeared in 1974.
4 He was in Marvel comics.
5 An X-Man is a mutant with superhuman powers.
6 It became a TV series in 1992.
7 Hugh Jackman, an Australian actor, played the part.
8 It explains the mysteries of Wolverine's past and how he became a mutant.

Writing

Exercise 2
Students' own answers.

Exercise 3
Students' own answers.

Unit 5

Vocabulary

Transportation

Exercise 1
1 bus 2 train 3 taxi 4 helicopter
5 boat 6 subway 7 truck 8 bike
9 airplane 10 motorcycle

Exercise 2
1 car 2 airplane 3 car 4 bike
5 train 6 bus

Grammar

Present progressive for future

Exercise 3
1 I'm going
2 Are we having
3 Is dad cooking
4 I'm not going
5 Jo isn't visiting
6 Mom is driving

Exercise 4
1 We're going to Mexico in January.
2 The party's starting at 8 o'clock.
3 I'm having a party with my friends next Friday.
4 My older brother is coming home at Easter.
5 We're finishing our history project tomorrow afternoon.
6 They're visiting their grandparents on Christmas day.

Exercise 5
1 I'm going to an English Language Summer School.
2 I'm flying (from Seoul).
3 I'm staying in Manly, Sydney.
4 I'm staying with an Australian family.
5 I'm staying for two weeks.

Future time expressions

Exercise 6
2 at 9 p.m. tonight
3 tomorrow morning
4 on Friday
5 this weekend
6 next week
7 next month

How long …? + take

Exercise 7
1 How long does it take to fly to the moon by spacecraft?
  It takes 3 days.
2 How long does it take to drive from Montreal to Ottawa?
  It takes about two hours.
3 How long does it take to walk one kilometer on foot?
  It takes 12 minutes.
4 How long does it take to fly from London, England to Sydney, Australia?
  It takes 22 hours.
5 How long does it take to travel from England to France by ferry?
  It takes 90 minutes.

Round-up

Exercise 8
1 train 2 airplane 3 subway
4 boat 5 bus 6 car

Exercise 9
1 are flying
2 are they arriving
3 are driving / going
4 are they staying
5 're taking
6 're staying
7 does it take
8 's making
9 are you doing
10 're going
11 're going

Communication

Making arrangements

Exercise 1
1 Let's do
2 How about
3 Why don't
4 a great idea
5 At what time
6 See you then

Exercise 2
B Good idea. What shall we do? 2
A Let's go to the swimming pool. 3
B I don't like swimming. Why don't we go rollerblading instead? 4
A That's a great idea. Where shall we meet? 5
B Let's meet at the entrance to the park. 6
A At what time? 7
B After lunch. At half past two. Is that OK? 8

Exercise 3
1 is it
2 It's
3 why don't we meet at

Exercise 4
Students' own answers.

Exercise 5
Students' own answers.

Skills

Reading

Exercise 1
John: an island near Scotland, U.K.
Emma: Arctic Circle, Canada
Anabeli: a small island near Croatia

Exercise 2
1 He goes to school by bike and ferry.
2 It takes about an hour.
3 She skis or goes on snowmobile.
4 She goes by airplane.
5 She goes twice a week.

Writing

Exercise 3
Students' own answers.

Unit 6

Vocabulary

Food and drink

Exercise 1
2 water 3 apple 4 milk 5 tomato
6 chicken 7 yogurt 8 beef
9 carrot 10 orange 11 bread
Hidden words: healthy food

Grammar

Countable / Uncountable nouns

Exercise 2
1 carrot 2 cookie 3 egg 4 tomato
5 bread 6 cheese 7 orange juice
8 rice 9 tuna

some / any

Exercise 3
1 some 2 a 3 some 4 any 5 a
6 any

Exercise 4
1 There isn't any water.
2 There are some onions.
3 There is some sugar.
4 There aren't any carrots.
5 There isn't any butter.
6 There is some vinegar.

a lot of / much / many

Exercise 5
1 I eat a lot of eggs.
2 I play a lot of sports.
3 We don't have much / a lot of time.
4 Do you have much / a lot of
   homework?
5 Sue doesn't have many cousins.
6 Does Louise eat much / a lot of meat?

How much …? / How many …?

Exercise 6
1 How many 2 How many 3 How
much 4 How many 5 How much
Students' own answers.

a little / a few

Exercise 7
1 How many carrots are there?
   There aren't many carrots.
   There are a few carrots.
2 How much cheese is there?
   There isn't much cheese.
   There's a little cheese.
3 How many mangoes are there?
   There aren't many mangoes.
   There are a few mangoes.
4 How much water is there?
   There's not much water.
   There's a little water.
5 How many apples are there?
   There aren't many apples.
   There are a few apples.

Round-up

Exercise 8
1 apple
2 carrot, potato
3 lamb, pork
4 cheese, yogurt
5 chocolate, cookie
6 orange juice, water

Exercise 9
1 some 2 some 3 any
4 a lot of 5 How much 6 a lot of
7 a lot of 8 many 9 How much
10 some 11 a lot of 12 much

Communication

Ordering food and drink

Exercise 1
1 I'd like
2 like to drink
3 I'll have
4 Large, please.
5 with tuna
6 Yes, please

Exercise 2
1 **Server** Can I help you?
  Boy Yes, please. I'd like a tuna
         sandwich.
  Server OK. And, would you like a
          drink?
  Boy Yes. I'll have a cup of coffee,
         please.
  Server Small or large?
  Boy Small, please.
2 **Server** What would you like to eat?
  Girl I'd like a ham pizza, please.
  Server Would you like chips with that?
  Girl No, thanks.
  Server And, what would you like to
          drink?
  Girl I'll have a small soda, please.

Exercise 3
1 eat 2 like 3 like 4 thanks
5 What 6 drink 7 have 8 please
9 for 10 'll

Exercise 4
1 baked potato with cheese, please
2 like a soda
3 like a hamburger with French fries
4 No, thanks
5 have a
6 sandwich
7 Yes, please
8 of milk

Exercise 5
Students' own answers.

Skills

Reading

Exercise 1
1 They have lunch at school.
2 They have burgers and French fries
   and healthy food like fruit and
   vegetables.
3 It is a lunch box.
4 In Japan.
5 There is sushi and other Japanese
   dishes.
6 They have a traffic light system. The
   food has labels with different colors.
7 It means a lot of fat, sugar, and salt.

Writing

Exercise 2
Students' own answers.

Unit 7

Vocabulary

Geography

Exercise 1
1 island 2 river 3 mountain
4 ocean 5 desert 6 continent
7 lake 8 volcano

Exercise 2
1 island 2 mountain 3 volcano
4 lake 5 Sea 6 Desert 7 Ocean
8 continent

Grammar

Comparative adjectives (Short adjectives)

Exercise 3
1 longer 2 happier 3 hotter
4 funnier 5 slower 6 larger
7 older 8 nicer

Exercise 4
1 I'm older than my brother.
2 It's hotter today than it was yesterday.
3 Cartoons are funnier than documentaries.
4 I'm taller than my sister.
5 The blue T-shirt is larger than the black T-shirt.
6 The movie has a happier ending than the book.
7 The Nile is longer than the Amazon.
8 Mr. York is nicer than Mrs. Hardwick.

Long adjectives

Exercise 5
1 more expensive than
2 more famous than
3 more intelligent than
4 more dangerous than
5 more popular than
6 more boring than

Irregular adjectives

Exercise 6
1 better 2 worse 3 further

Exercise 7
1 cheaper 2 more relaxed
3 friendlier 4 easier 5 further
6 better 7 nearer

as … as

Exercise 8
1 Adam Sandler isn't as funny as Owen Wilson.
  Owen Wilson isn't as funny as Adam Sandler.
2 Matt Damon isn't as famous as Johnny Depp.
  Johnny Depp isn't as famous as Matt Damon.
3 Fanny Lu isn't as good looking as Paulina Rubio.
  Paulina Rubio isn't as good looking as Fanny Lu.
4 Robinho isn't as talented as Ji-Sung Park.
  Ji-Sung Park isn't as talented as Robinho.
5 Anne Hathaway isn't as tall as Keira Knightley.
  Keira Knightley isn't as tall as Anne Hathaway.

less … than

Exercise 9
1 English is less difficult than Portuguese.
2 Baseball is less popular than basketball.
3 Movie tickets are less expensive than concert tickets.
4 English is less important than science.
5 Danny Minogue is less famous than Kylie Minogue.

Exercise 10
1 English isn't as difficult as Portuguese.
2 Baseball isn't as popular as basketball.
3 Movie tickets aren't as expensive as concert tickets.
4 English isn't as important as science.
5 Danny Minogue isn't as famous as Kylie Minogue.

Round-up

Exercise 11
1 bigger than 2 as hot as 3 drier
4 larger 5 as deep as 6 longer
7 higher 8 less high than
9 more famous

Communication

Asking for tourist information

Exercise 1
1 How much 2 does it open
3 as many 4 Where is it 5 can I get
6 as fast as

Exercise 2
2 a 3 e 4 f 5 d 6 b

Exercise 3
1 It's on Liberty Island.
2 You can take the ferry from Battery Park.
3 They are $12 for adults, $5 for children, and $10 for over 60s.
4 No, there isn't.
5 It's open from 8:30 a.m. to 6:15 p.m.

Exercise 4
Students' own answers.

Skills

Reading

Exercise 1
1 Salvador 2 Chapada Diamantina
3 Abrolhos

Exercise 2
1 It is in the northeast of Brazil.
2 Salvador is the capital.
3 They can see beautiful, colorful houses and monuments from the 17th century.
4 It lasts seven days and seven nights.
5 It is in the center of Bahia.
6 They can go walking, mountain biking, swimming, and snorkelling.
7 It is off the south coast of Bahia.
8 It is famous for whales and its colorful, exotic fish and spectacular coral formations.

Writing

Exercise 3
Students' own answers.

Unit 8

Vocabulary

Feelings and emotions

Exercise 1
2 g 3 f 4 h 5 a 6 b 7 e 8 c

Grammar

Superlative adjectives (Short adjectives)

Exercise 2
2 prettiest 3 tallest 4 nicest
5 cleverest 6 heaviest 7 oldest
8 saddest

Exercise 3
1 Tim is the tallest.
2 Jess is the fastest.
3 Marius is the shortest.
4 Jess is the oldest.
5 Jess is the lightest.
6 Marius is the strongest.
7 Tim is the youngest.

Long and irregular adjectives

Exercise 4
1 best 2 most fashionable
3 most famous

Exercise 5
1 the most popular 2 the best
3 the most exciting 4 cheapest
5 furthest 6 the angriest
7 the worst

Exercise 6
Students' own answers.

Comparative / Superlative

Exercise 7
1 better 2 the most embarrassing
3 more interesting
4 the most expensive 5 stronger
6 the funniest

the least

Exercise 8
1 the least confident
2 the least popular 3 the least difficult
4 the least expensive

Round-up

Exercise 9
1 fastest 2 longest 3 tallest
4 most expensive 5 most dangerous

Communication

Making a phone call

Exercise 1
1 leave a message 2 return my call
3 My number is 4 speak with
5 Who's calling 6 for you

Exercise 2
2 d 3 a 4 e 5 b

Exercise 3
1 Hello. Where's Tanya?
2 What's her cell phone number?
3 I can't meet her at the movie theater tonight.
4 Yes, please. Can you ask her to return my call after six o'clock?
5 No, she doesn't. It's 787-632-1634.
6 Thanks. Bye.

Exercise 4
Students' own answers.

Skills

Reading

Exercise 1
1 You can see George Washington, Thomas Jefferson, Abraham Lincoln, and Theodore Roosevelt.
2 They are the largest group of sculptures in the world.
3 Doane Robinson had the idea.
4 He wanted to attract more tourists to the area.
5 Gutzon Borglum and his son created them.
6 They created them between 1927 and 1941.
7 400 people helped them.
8 More than 2 million tourists visit it every year.

Writing

Exercise 2
The Grand Canyon is in Arizona. It is a glass walkway over the deepest canyon in the world. It is 1,200 meters above the floor of the Grand Canyon. The Hualapi Native American people built it in 2006. Tourists can walk on the glass and look down at the canyon. It is the highest walkway in the world and it is one of the biggest tourist attractions in the south-west of America.

Exercise 3
Students' own answers.